ad usum
Michael P. Joyce, cs

CONSECRATED LIFE

CASES, COMMENTARY, DOCUMENTS, READINGS

BY

SR. ROSE MCDERMOTT, SSJ

Canon Law Society of America
108 North Payne Street, Suite C
Alexandria, VA 22314-2906

D1528506

ISBN: 1-932208-13-5
SAN: 237-6296

The Canon Law Society of America's programs and publications are designed solely to help canonists maintain their professional competence. In dealing with specific canonical matters, the canonist using Canon Law Society of America publications or orally conveyed information should also research original sources of authority.

The views and opinions expressed in this publication are those of the individual authors and do not represent the views of the Canon Law Society of America (CLSA), its Board of Governors, Staff or members. The CLSA does not endorses the views or opinions expressed by the individual authors. The publisher and authors specifically disclaim any liability, loss or risk, personal or otherwise, which is incurred as a consequence, directly or indirectly, of the use, reliance, or application of any of the contents of this publication.

Canons cited in this text are used with permission and taken from the *Code of Canon Law Latin-English Edition New English Translation*, Washington: Canon Law Society of America, 1999.

Canon Law Society of America
108 North Payne Street, Suite C
Alexandria, VA 22314
2006

TABLE OF CONTENTS

Part I

The Authority of the Apostolic See and the Diocesan Bishop over Institutes of Consecrated Life

CASES

Part II

The Authority of Major Superiors and Chapters in Institutes of Consecrated Life

CASES

PREFACE

The work contains samples of issues addressed by the author in the Latin church over a period of twenty-five years in serving individual members and major superiors of institutes of consecrated life, diocesan bishops and the latter's chancery personnel. While the cases address religious institutes, they are applicable to societies of apostolic life, *mutatis mutandis,* since the societies live community life in common in the spirit of the evangelical counsels or through sacred bonds described in their proper laws. In each of the cases the author attempts to combine canonical expertise with a pastoral approach, convinced that canonists need employ both for effective service to members of these institutes and societies as well as to those with authority over these stable forms of life within the Church.

Hopefully, the text will benefit canonists serving in chanceries and tribunals who have taken a course in consecrated life, but lacked the time or opportunity to apply their theoretical knowledge in a seminar on selected issues. Frequently their diocesan bishops or major superiors call on them to address and resolve such issues in their respective dioceses. Diocesan bishops and major superiors of institutes of consecrated life should also find the text helpful, since they deal with such issues within the context of their ministries to members and institutes of consecrated life.

The author owes a depth of gratitude to Barbara Anne Cusack, J.C.D., Chancellor of the Archdiocese of Milwaukee; Sister Sharon Holland, I.H.M., J.C.D., Official of the Congregation for Institutes of Consecrated Life and Societies of Apostolic Life; and Rev. Francis G. Morrisey, O.M.I., J.C.D., Professor of Canon Law at St. Paul University, Ottawa, for the time and expertise they so generously offered in reviewing the text and offering wise suggestions.

****

Rose McDermott, SSJ

v

INTRODUCTION

Some years ago, a colleague shared his experience of studying canon law as a seminarian. He and some of his companions found the cases with which the professor illustrated his lectures to be outrageous. Among themselves they ridiculed these creative inventions. Then, about five years after ordination, he admitted that all of the case characters had presented themselves in his parish office.

Those cases, most probably, were stories told in the course of teaching marriage law. However, those who have become expert Tribunal officials are, understandably, often still novices in the world of religious law. The cases which are used as a methodology in *Consecrated Life: Cases, Commentary, Documents and Readings,* like those of the marriage law professor did not have to be invented. The author's experience has provided a broad repertoire. And, if they are presented in less colorful language than those of the seminary professor, it is only a sign of their sober reality. Bishops, religious superiors, canonists and vicars for religious will all recognize in these scenarios, the faces of persons they have met and tried to help.

The important art of asking questions is one of the important elements highlighted in the book's presentation. It is an occupational hazard for many of us to feel that we must have answers, and have them fairly quickly. This is indeed desirable, but risks not having understood the question. The queries offered after each case remind us that not all of the facts are immediately evident when the tale is told. This partial telling of the tale may be conscious or unconscious; it may be due to unawareness that something is important, a presumption that certain facts are obvious, or calculated to elicit the desired answer. Still, everything can change suddenly if it becomes clear that the institute is diocesan, not pontifical; that the religious is in temporary, not perpetual vows; that the religious is ordained; the monastery is in a federation; or the institute is regulated by the canons for the Eastern Churches. The need to ask questions challenges our shortness of time and patience, but gradually yields the full picture so that a just and equitable solution can be proposed.

Another aspect raised by the repeated case questions is the necessity of dealing in an integrated way with both universal law (the Code) and proper law (Constitutions, Directories, Chapter Handbooks, Federation Statutes, etc.). In dealing with institutes of consecrated life (religious or secular) and societies of apostolic life, it is not enough for a canonist to know the Code. Since different congregations and institutes have different norms in their Constitutions, it cannot be presumed that everything is settled by the canons, or done in one institute as it is done in another.

The legitimate diversity introduced by the revision of the Code, in light of the Second Vatican Council's recognition of distinctive charisms, has made it crucial that proper law be consulted in religious matters. As the commentaries provided on each case point out, it is also essential to pursue other parts of the Code, beyond the canons proper to consecrated life. Questions about councils or chapters can send one to Book I on seeking counsel, on collegial bodies, and on conducting elections. Economic matters may often open up the intricacies of Book V. The sensitive question of dismissal may send one to canons of Book VII on administrative recourse.

In addition to demonstrating canonical complexities, the commentaries demonstrate, by their approach, the "mutuality" of relationship between institutes and bishops, which must mark ecclesial communion. Whether preparing a case for canonical consultation or being consulted, the cases and commentaries can serve one in preparing the presentation or approaching a fully informed solution. Actual or sample documents provide a concrete aid in knowing how to proceed. Further, the select bibliographical references with each topic, will serve those who need to pursue a particular topic in greater depth, and with the ever-present diversity of canonical opinion.

With this much said, it must be added that the law alone is not enough. As the author points out in the Preface, canonical expertise must be combined with a pastoral approach. Over twenty years ago, the *Preface to the Latin Edition* of the Code drew attention to this balance. The 1967 Synod's principles, given to guide the revision of the canons, had stated in number three:

> "To foster the pastoral care of souls as much as possible, the new law, besides the virtue of justice, is to take cognizance of charity, temperance, humaneness and moderation, whereby equity is to be pursued not only in the application of the laws by pastors of souls but also in the legislation itself. Hence unduly rigid norms are to be set aside and rather recourse is to be taken to exhortations and persuasions where there is not need of a strict observance of the law on account of the public good and general ecclesiastical discipline."

In line with this, one can easily transfer to the professional canonist, Pope Benedict XVI's words regarding those engaged in the Church's charitable organizations: "Individuals who care for those in need must first be professionally competent. [...] Yet while professional competence is a primary, fundamental requirement, it is not of itself sufficient. We are dealing with human beings, and human beings always need something more than technical proper care. They need humanity. They need heartfelt concern." (*Deus Caritas Est,* n. 31-a)

May the Church be blessed with new professional canonists, experts in the law for consecrated life, and in heartfelt human concern.

Sr. Sharon Holland, IHM

Part I

The Authority of the Apostolic See and the Diocesan Bishop over Institutes of Consecrated Life

Canon 576

The Church teaches that the evangelical counsels based on the teaching and example of Christ are a divine gift that it is obliged to preserve through God's grace (c. 575). To this end, the Church is intrusted with the interpretation of the evangelical counsels and has done so through the years through theological and canonical norms (cc. 576, 599-601). Likewise, it has promulgated universal laws and approved proper laws that preserve and foster these counsels by persons called and committed to living them. While only the Apostolic See can constitute new forms of consecrated life, diocesan bishops discern new gifts and assist promoters to express them in statutes guided by the general norms of the code (c. 605).

Both the Congregation for Institutes of Consecrated Life and Societies of Apostolic Life (CICLSAL) and a diocesan bishop in his own territory can erect institutes of consecrated life (religious institutes, secular institutes) and societies of apostolic life in the Latin church. If erected or approved as such by CICLSAL, they are institutes of pontifical right accountable to that same congregation regarding internal governance and discipline (c. 593); if erected by a diocesan bishop, they are institutes of diocesan right and remain under the diocesan bishop's special care (c. 594). The diocesan bishop has a special vigilance over a *sui iuris* monastery which does not have another major superior besides its own moderator and is not associated with another institute of religious in such a way that the superior of that institute possesses true power over the monastery determined by the constitutions (cc. 615; 625 §2; 628 §2, 1°; 637; 638 §4;; 688 §2; 699 §2).

At the time of the erection the constitutions of an institute of consecrated life are approved by the appropriate ecclesiastical authority (CICLSAL or a diocesan bishop). These same authorities would confirm changes legitimately introduced into the constitutions (c. 587 §2) and address affairs of greater importance affecting the whole institute and exceeding the power of internal authority. A diocesan bishop, however, could not decide on affairs that are reserved to the Apostolic See (c. 593 §1).

1

Members of institutes of consecrated life are obliged to remain faithful to their sacred patrimony and sound traditions (c. 578), as well as the fundamental norms directing the course of the institute set down in constitutions (c. 587 §1). Ecclesiastical authorities have an obligation to see that these institutes grow and flourish in the spirit of the founder or foundress and their sacred traditions (c. 576). Local ordinaries are obliged to preserve and safeguard the autonomy of life of these institutes (c. 586). Finally, since the state of those who profess the evangelical counsels in these institutes belongs to the life and holiness of the Church, all of the Christian faithful are obliged to foster and promote this vocation (c. 574 §1).

The Second Vatican Council has renewed two ancient forms of consecrated life: the eremitic or anchoritic life (*LG* 43, *PC* 1, *AG* 18, 40) and the Order of Virgins (*SC* 80, *AA* 19). While two canons describe these forms of consecrated life (cc. 603, 604), these men and women are not members of institutes of consecrated life, but are under the authority and direction of the diocesan bishop or one delegated by him. As consecrated persons in the Church, the hermits and consecrated virgins provide for their present and future needs.

Case 1
Entrusting a Parish to a Clerical Religious Institute
Canons 520, 678 §1, 681, 682 §

Case

A major superior of a clerical religious institute offers to send three of his members to administer a parish in a diocese. The bishop seems willing to accept this offer and asks his canonist to investigate the matter and draw up an agreement for his review. What issues should the canonist investigate and what should he include in the contract?

QUESTIONS PERTINENT TO THE CASE

1. How large is the religious institute; is it of pontifical or diocesan right?
2. Does the nature and purpose of the institute provide for this type of apostolic service for the members of the institute?
3. Has the institute a good record in other dioceses regarding witness to consecrated life, service in parochial ministry, and cooperation with the diocesan bishop?
4. Is the major superior aware of and does he abide by the norms recommended by the United States Conference of Catholic Bishops (USCCB) for presenting religious for ministries and apostolic service?
5. Can the major superior assure the diocesan bishop that the institute will administer the parish with stability?
6. Is the major superior prepared to present one of the members as parish priest, pastor, of the parish; can he assure a replacement if a term of office is in place?
7. Is the compensation package, i.e., stipend, pension plan arrangements, health care benefits, holidays, the duration of the contract, and provision for ownership of property and temporal goods amenable to the major superior and his financial officer?
8. Does the major superior have any *sine qua non* provisions that must be honored by the diocese as part of the contractual arrangement?
9. Will only the members serving the parish be present in the rectory; does the major superior have any other designs for this local community of priests?
10. Are the members assigned to the parish willing to abide by the particular laws of the diocese for parish ministry and liturgical celebrations?

3

Can. 520 §1. A juridic person is not to be a pastor. With the consent of the competent superior, however, a diocesan bishop, but not a diocesan administrator, can entrust a parish to a clerical religious institute or clerical society of apostolic life, even by erecting it in a church of the institute or society, with the requirement, however, that one presbyter is to be the pastor of the parish or, if the pastoral care is entrusted to several *in solidum,* the moderator as mentioned in can. 517 §1.

§2. The entrusting of a parish mentioned in §1 can be made either perpetually or for a specific, predetermined time. In either case it is to be made by means of a written agreement between the diocesan bishop and the competent superior of the institute or society, which expressly and accurately defines, among other things, the work to be accomplished, the persons to be assigned to the parish, and the financial arrangements.

Can. 678 §1. Religious are subject to the power of bishops whom they are bound to follow with devoted submission and reverence in those matters which regard the care of souls, the public exercise of divine worship, and other works of the apostolate.

Can. 681 §1. Works which a diocesan bishop entrusts to religious are subject to the authority and direction of the same bishop, without prejudice to the right of religious superiors according to the norm of can. 678, §§2 and 3.

§2. In these cases, the diocesan bishop and the competent superior of the institute are to draw up a written agreement which, among other things, is to define expressly and accurately those things which pertain to the work to be accomplished, the members to be devoted to it, and economic matters.

Can. 682 §1. If it concerns conferring an ecclesiastical office in a diocese upon some religious, the diocesan bishop appoints the religious, with the competent superior making the presentation, or at least assenting to the appointment.

§2. A religious can be removed from the office entrusted to him or her at the discretion either of the entrusting authority after having informed the religious superior or of the superior after having informed the one entrusting; neither requires the consent of the other.

COMMENTARY

After an initial interview with the major superior, the canonist should call the diocese wherein the provincial house is located. The chancellor or vicar for clergy could assist in giving an evaluation of the witness and ministerial activity of the members of that particular religious institute in the diocese and perhaps in other dioceses. It would be well to inquire as to their zeal in their commitments and the number of members in the province as they undertake the administration of another parish. The canonist should inquire of the major superior or the vicar for clergy if the religious institute employs the "Proposed Guidelines on the Assessment of Clergy and Religious for Assignment" published by the then National Conference of Catholic Bishops (NCCB).

If all seems favorable in that diocese and the canonist is ready to prepare the agreement or contract for the review of both the diocesan bishop and the major superior, he should familiarize himself with canons 520, 678, 681, 682, and 683. The diocesan bishop is entrusting the religious institute with the administration of a parish. The religious remain subject to him regarding the care of souls, apostolic activity, and public liturgical worship (c. 678 §1), but they also remain subject to their major superior regarding their obligations of religious life in accord with the nature, spirit, and ends of the institute while serving the parish (c. 678 §2).

Canon 520 §2 and 681 §2 provide that the agreement contain a description of the work to be done, the members assigned, and any financial arrangements between the parties. The agreement should be made between the diocesan bishop representing the diocese and the major superior representing the institute. Before the canonist begins to craft a new agreement, it may be well to see if the diocese or neighboring ones have copies of such agreements. The contract should provide a time at which the contract expires and is renewable as well as a provision that either party (diocesan bishop or major superior), having given ample notice, can withdraw from the agreement. These measures protect both the interests of the diocese and those of the religious institute.

The number of religious (priests, deacons, or brothers) provided in the agreement for work in the parish is important. In the event that one becomes ill or is reassigned to another ministry, there is reassurance of a replacement. It is necessary that one priest be presented to the diocesan bishop for the office of pastor (cc. 520 §1, 682 §1) or as moderator of an *in solidum* team (c. 517 §1). If the major superior has designs on having other members other than those working in the parish (students, campus ministers) reside in the rectory, this should be made clear to the diocesan bishop. There should be some provision regarding their board, etc.

The major superior should be informed as to the stipend that religious priests receive for parochial service; often it is the same stipend as that of the diocesan priests in the parishes. What are the provisions for health and retirement benefits for religious priests serving in a parish?

Some religious institutes of men ask that the house be erected as a juridic person (c. 609), in order that the local community has representation at the provincial chapter and other rights accorded religious due to the canonical status of a house in the institute's proper law. The house is erected by the major superior competent in the proper law of the institute with the prior written consent of the diocesan bishop (c. 609 §1).

Clear distinctions should be made between the temporal goods belonging to the parish and the temporal goods of the religious institute. There should be a written understanding as to diocesan collections, stole fees, and Mass offerings, as well as any special collection permitted the religious for their institute (retirement or education of members, building fund, etc.). Provisions should be made in the contract regarding items such as transportation, vacation, sick leave, and religious life obligations. There should be clarity regarding parish and institute expenses such as utilities (water, electricity, gas, phone, etc.).

There should be an accurate description of the work to be done in the parish, particularly the role of the pastor. The religious are accountable while performing parochial ministry to the diocesan bishop and are obligated to obey the particular law of the diocese. But they are also responsible to their major superior in carrying out their ministry according to the nature, spirit, and purpose of the institute as described in the proper law of the institute (cc. 678 §1, §2).

HELPFUL REFERENCES

- DePaolis, Velasio. "Schema of an Agreement for the Assignment of a Parish to Religious." *Consecrated Life* 12:1-2 (1986) 129-146; 218-242.

- Hite, Jordan. "Mutual Rights and Obligations of Major Superiors Regarding Public Ministry." *Bulletin on Issues of Religious Law* 14 (Spring 1997) 1-8.

- NCCB. "Proposed Guidelines on the Assessment of Clergy and Religious for Assignment." *Canon Law Newsletter* (March 1994) 3, 6-7.

- Palmieri, Rev. Msgr. Alexander. "Parishes Entrusted to the Care of Religious: Starting Afresh from Christ." *CLSA Proceedings* (October 7-10, 2002) 209-240.

SAMPLE OF AN AGREEMENT

BETWEEN A DIOCESE AND A RELIGIOUS INSTITUTE

(In his article cited below, Msgr. Palmieri recommended the following draft of an agreement and gave the author permission to use it as a sample with appropriate modifications):

Agreement Between the Roman Catholic Diocese of _____
　　and the _____Province of _____Order

　　The Diocese of _____ of the Latin Rite (Diocese) represented by Bishop _____ and the _____ Province, a clerical religious institute of pontifical right (Institute) represented by Very Rev. _____, Provincial Superior, accept the following terms of an agreement relating to the Parish of _____ (Parish).

　　1. Having consulted the Presbyteral Council of the Diocese and having secured the consent of the Provincial Superior, the Diocese entrusts to the Institute in accordance with this agreement the Parish, located at _____, in the Diocese.
　　2. The Institute will administer the Parish in spiritual and temporal matters in accordance with the prescriptions of canon law and Diocesan norms, directives, and practices, except in what concerns the autonomy and observances of the Institute according to its nature and purpose as specified in its approved proper law.
　　3. The Parish with its temporalities and property, real and personal, is entrusted to the Institute in accord with the terms of this agreement. It remains a Diocesan entity in accord with the existing canon law as well as in accord with the civil law of the state of _____ . Repairs needed for the preparation and maintenance of living quarters for the members of the Institute assigned to the Parish will be provided by the Parish. Modifications needed for the work of the members of the Institute in residence will be provided by the Institute, all necessary permissions having been previously obtained from the Diocese.
　　4. All income from any Parish functions, Parish related activities, or bequests/legacies to the Parish, belongs to the Parish. The Institute may appeal to the parishioners for one special collection each year, not to conflict with the schedule of Diocesan collections or regular Parish collections. The Institute agrees not to engage in any other solicitation of funds, bequests or legacies, direct or indirect, for the Institute itself without the specific authorization of the Bishop.
　　5. The Institute as such does not assume the responsibility for past or future debts of the Parish. Neither does the Parish as such assume the responsibility for any past or future debts of the Institute.
　　6. The Institute agrees to staff the Parish with a minimum of one and a maximum of two full-time priests. One of the priests will serve as pastor. The

appointment of the pastor and parochial vicar(s) as well as the termination of their assignment will be in accord with the prescriptions of canon law.

7. Each of the full-time priests assigned to the Parish will be entitled to compensation and benefits provided for religious priests who serve as pastors or parochial vicars. Schedule is attached to this agreement.

8. According to Parish needs and resources, the Institute may assign a maximum of two brothers to the Parish staff for general and particular work of the Parish ministry.

9. Full-time brother(s) assigned to the Parish will be entitled to the compensation and benefits provided to religious brothers assigned to the Diocese. The schedule is attached to this agreement.

10. If the Institute assigns additional members to the community of the Parish house in accord with proper law, the maintenance and support of these members shall be the responsibility of the Institute.

11. One automobile to be used by the staff solely for parochial services may be purchased and maintained by the Parish. Premiums for the insurance for Parish-owned automobile(s) will be the responsibility of the Parish. All other vehicles used by the parish staff are the responsibility of the Institute.

12. Any item not included in this Agreement relative to the administration of the Parish shall be regulated in accord with the prescriptions of canon law as well as by Diocesan norms and practices.

13. This agreement between the Diocese and the Institute shall be binding for a period of three years beginning _____ and ending on _____ . It can be terminated at any time only by the consent of both parties. It shall be renewed automatically every three years, unless written notice be given by either party six months before the original or any subsequent renewal date of the Agreement.

14. The interpretation or application of any part of the Agreement is to be made in accord with canon law, the norms and practices of the Diocese, and the proper law of the Institute.

15. In order to delete, alter, or add to any of the provisions of the Agreement, the consent of both parties is required. Such deletions, alterations, or additions shall conform to canon law, Diocesan norms and regualtions, as well as the Institute's proper law.

_____   _____
Bishop of _____   Provincial Superior

_____   SEAL
Date

8

Case 2

The Erection of a Religious Institute of Diocesan Right
Canon 579

Case

Four women living in one of the parish convents and offering religious instruction to the Hispanic children approach the diocesan bishop. They petition to become a diocesan religious institute. They explain that they have left their secular lives and positions to assist the pastor in return for the use of the convent and a small stipend. Two of the women speak Spanish fluently, but seem disinclined to learn English. The women have no background in religious education or catechetics. One of them gave up a stable position as a legal secretary to join the others in parish service. What would be some issues the canonist representing the bishop would need to discuss with these women regarding their request?

QUESTIONS PERTINENT TO THE CASE

1. How did these women come together, how long have they been together in this diocese, and what is the canonical status of each?
2. Who seems to be the charismatic leader among the women, and what is her vision of the institute, i.e., its nature, spirit, and end?
3. Does this vision seem to duplicate the nature, spirit, and purpose of another institute already present and functioning in the diocese?
4. Do these women understand the essential elements of religious life; are there some experienced women religious available to assist them in the practice of religious life and with guidelines or statutes for review by the diocesan bishop?
5. What were the women's secular positions, and how are they managing their finances and spiritual and temporal necessities?
6. Does the diocese have requirements (educational and otherwise) for those engaged in catechetics; do any of the women have teaching experience and/or degrees or certification for teaching catechetics?
7. Is the religious education offered in Spanish; is it in keeping with diocesan norms for catechetical education; are provisions made in the program for non-Hispanic children?
8. Is there a strong Hispanic presence in the diocese willing to draw on the

services of these women?

9. Are the women willing to learn English and adapt to the educational program in the diocese?
10. Do the women understand the canonical steps in becoming a religious institute?
11. Have the women attracted any additional members since their beginnings?
12. Is the nature and purpose of the institute useful for the mission of the diocese?
13. What is their present status; have they been recognized or established as an association of the faithful in the diocese or are they simply an association *de facto*?

THE LAW

> Can 576 It is for the competent authority of the Church to interpret the evangelical counsels, to direct their practice by laws, and by canonical approbation to establish the stable forms of living deriving from the, and also, for its part, to take care that the institutes grow and flourish according to the spirit of the founders and sound traditions.

> Can. 579 Diocesan bishops, each in his own territory, can erect institutes of consecrated life by formal decree, provided that the Apostolic See has been consulted.

COMMENTARY

The canonist representing the diocesan bishop should meet with these women who have already formed a *de facto* private association of the faithful (c. 299 §1) with the intention of its developing into a diocesan religious institute (c. 579). During the initial interview, the canonist should ask questions similar to those above in order to procure pertinent information for the bishop. It would be important to assess the canonical status of these women so as to determine the presence of invalidating impediments which would preclude their becoming religious. For example, are they baptized Catholics and not bound by the bond of marriage or incorporation in an institute of consecrated life (cc. 597, 643). It is well to keep a file on the association and each of the women in the office of the chancery or that of the vicar for consecrated life.

It would be important to interview the charismatic leader or founder as to her vision of the shape that the fledgling beginnings will take. Since most members of the Christian faithful do not readily recognize the canonical distinctions between institutes of consecrated life (religious institutes (c. 607), secular institutes (cc. 710-712) and societies of apostolic life (c. 731), the canonist should listen carefully so as to determine which form of consecrated life is envisioned. If the leader seems to describe the nature, spirit, and goal of a religious institute or already in existence, then the foundress should be advised of the same by the canonist. The canonist should encourage both the foundress and the other associates to apply for admission to that institute. CICLSAL discourages foundations that duplicate those already approved.

If the vision of the founder seems somewhat similar to the traditional spirituality of an already approved institute (Benedictine, Franciscan, Carmelite, Dominican), the group, if it continues to flourish, must assume a title that clearly distinguishes it from the already approved entity whose tradition it reflects (*Roman Replies* (1995) 9). If the spirituality does not seem to replicate already approved institutes or societies, it would be important to question the foundress with the companions as to their understanding of the essential elements of religious life: commitment to a life of the evangelical counsels and common life. The women should give some indication that they are living in the spirit of the counsels, i.e., through promises or private vows. Likewise, they should live a common life in peace and harmony.

The canonist should carefully explain to the women the steps involved in becoming a diocesan religious institute. Ordinarily, the group will advance from a *de facto* association of the faithful (c. 299 §1) to a private association with it statutes reviewed and approved by the diocesan bishop (c. 322 §2), to a public association of the faithful (cc. 312 §1, 3°, 313, 314). Each of these steps is crucial for the potential institute, and should be taken slowly, since once approval is given, it is difficult to retract. These steps afford the diocesan bishop time to study the association, its doctrinal and liturgical orthodoxy, and to make decisions for its canonical status based on: 1) its nature, spirit, and purpose described in the statutes; 2) its ability to attract members; and 3) its financial stability. Likewise, the women should show a commitment to the mission of the Church in that particular diocese. The diocesan bishop or his canonist should visit the association periodically, checking on its progress in these areas, and keeping the file updated (c. 305 §1). The association should be cautioned as to promoting itself publicly as a religious institute through vocabulary and signs such as a religious habit until it is approved as such.

Prior to the erection of a diocesan religious institute, the diocesan bishop must consult the Apostolic See, i.e., CICLSAL. This congregation will examine the several aspects of the association as described in the rescript attached to this case. Primarily, it will review the doctrine and uniqueness of its spirit, its ability to attract new members, its financial stability, and the constitutions. The congregation will reply to the diocesan bishop recommending or not recommending his erection of the association as a diocesan religious institute or society of apostolic life. In the latter case, it will give reasons for its unfavorable response. While the diocesan bishop would not seem to be bound by the consultation with the CICLSAL, it would be unwise to proceed with the canonical erection of the religious institute if the reasons presented by that dicastery are prudent. It should be remembered that once erected by the diocesan bishop, the religious institute becomes a public juridic person by the law itself with permanence in the Church (c. 634 §1).

11

- Holland, Sharon, I.H.M. "New Institutes, Mergers, and Suppression." *Procedural Handbook for Institutes of Consecrated Life and Societies of Apostolic Life.* Washington, D.C.: Canon Law Society of America: 31-39.

- Joyce, Michael P., C.M. and Rose McDermott, S.S.J. "Canon 579 - Erection of a Diocesan Institute." *CLSA Advisory Opinions* (1984-1993) 159-163.

- Congregation for Religious and Secular Institutes. "Documents and Information to be Sent to the Holy See in View of Canonical Erection of an Institute of Diocesan Right." *Canon Law Digest* 7: 457-459:

  1. Names of the Founder/foundress and of the first Superior General, with a brief *curriculum vitae* of each.
  2. A historical-juridical account of the Institute from its beginnings, a copy of the document by which the ecclesiastical authority approved the Institute should be included.
  3. Six copies of the Constitutions and the Directory of the Institute, revised in accordance with the *Code of Canon Law.* Two copies of the book of prayers, ceremonial, etc.
  4. Photographs of the religious dress of a professed and of a novice.
  5. Up-to-date statistics of membership (personal data in regard to each individual member), place and diocese in which the members are living and working; works of the Institute.
  6. An account of the patrimony of the Institute, including a declaration of debts.
  7. A statement regarding each of the following points:
     a) any facts of an extraordinary nature with reference to the Institute, such as visions, etc.
     b) particular devotions or exercise of piety, specific to the Institute.
     c) whether in the Diocese of origin of the Institute there exists already any other Institute with the same name and purpose.
  8. Testimonial letters from the Ordinaries of those dioceses in which the Institute is represented. Such letters are to be sent directly to the Holy See, together with the opinion of the same Bishops about the following items, namely: usefulness, stability, discipline of the Institute, formation of members, government, administration of goods, liturgical and sacramental dimension, a sense of being with the Church, particularly in regard to the observance of ecclesiastical discipline as expressed in the common law of the Church and in the diocesan directives, collaboration.

9. Please forward to the Cash Office of the Congregation for Religious and Secular Institutes a deposit equivalent to $200.00 US $ on account for the expenses of the entire process.

Rome, 1988

- Guidelines Concerning the Approval of a Public Association Composed of Celibate Men and Women in View of Becoming an Institute of Consecrated Life of Diocesan Right

1. Before erecting the Association it is important, among other things, to specify carefully its charism, it spirituality and its apostolate, and to include them in the Constitutions which are to be approved by the Bishop of the principal seat of the Association "ad experimentum" for three or more years.

2. In the Decree of erection of the Association it is important to include the following phrase: "We erect the public Association of Christ's Faithful, called _____ in view of being erected in the future an Institute of consecrated life of diocesan right. It is formed up of two principal separate branches including: a) celibate consecrated men (clerics and lay men), b) celibate consecrated women; the members of these branches pronounce private vows of chastity, poverty and obedience. Married couples may form part of the Association only as "associated members" (Cf. Post-Synodal Apostolic Exhortation: "Vita Consecrata," n. 62)."

They should have a separate Statute, including their own organization and their relation with the Association.

3. The two principal branches have their own juridical structure, with a President having some authority over all the Association, elected in a General Assembly. The President is assisted by his Council formed up of the Superiors General and the General Councils of both branches.

4. The members may: 1) have their own "period of provation," in common or separately; 2) pronounce private vows; 3) have their own government, keeping in mind the number of perpetually professed members; 4) establish their houses in other dioceses, without erecting a new Association.

This structure will facilitate the regularization of the canonical position of the individual members when the new Institute will be canonically established.

5. The vows pronounced in the Association are only private vows and they are not considered as "religious vows".

13

6. The Bishops of the dioceses where the Association is present are to follow and to watch over the formation of the candidates, the government of the Association and the administration of its temporal goods.

7. Clerics are incardinate in the diocese where they have their domicile; dimissorial letters to receive Holy Orders are given by the Bishop of the diocese where the clerics are formed.

8. When the Association has given proof of its maturity, with at least 40 consecrated members of whom the major part would be in perpetual vows, so that it may have its own Superiors and formators, the Association may be erected an Institute of consecrated life of diocesan right.

In this case, the praxis of the Congregation for Institutes of Consecrated Life and Societies of Apostolic Life is as follows: the Bishops of the principal seat of the Association will forward his petition to the same Congregation, together with other required documents. If all the elements for a consecrated life required by canons 573 ss., are included in the Constitutions, the same Congregation will authorize the Bishop of the principal seat of the Association to recognize the Association as an *"Institute of consecrated life of diocesan right,"* and to approve the Constitutions normally for five years "ad experimentum," after having corrected them according to the eventual observations indicated by the same Dicastery.

Vatican, 2002

DECREE OF ERECTION:
A RELIGIOUS INSTITUTE OF DIOCESAN RIGHT

Prot. n. _____

_____, the general superior of the public association of the faithful known as _____ in the diocese of _____, petitions that the association be established as a religious institute of diocesan right.

Having studied the petition, the advice accorded me by the Congregation for Institutes of Consecrated Life and Societies of Apostolic Life in accord with canon 579 of the *Code of Canon Law* and reviewed and approved the proposed constitutions, I hereby erect this public association of the faithful as a diocesan religious institute.

As a religious institute of diocesan right, the institute enjoys juridic personality and autonomy of life in accord with canons 586 and 634. It remains subject to the authority of the diocesan bishop in all those matters prescribed in the *Code of Canon Law* for religious institutes of diocesan right.

May the blessings of God descend on and remain with each member of this religious institute who has given a total gift of self in service to God's people.

_____
(Name)
Bishop of _____

(Date)_____

Case 3

The Erection of Parts of an Institute of Consecrated Life
Canon 581

Case

A superior general sought the advice of a canonist as the institute prepared for its ordinary general chapter of affairs. The superior explained to the canonist that the institute has a thriving region in South America with the potential for many vocations. At present, the region is governed by a regional superior appointed and delegated by the superior general with accountability to the general administration. The superior general and council recognize the need to enhance the structure of the region to a province with a major superior and council, a novitiate and formation program, and greater financial autonomy. However, the constitutions of the institute provide that "the superior general with the consent of the council can divide the institute into regions." What must she do in order to erect a province?

QUESTIONS PERTINENT TO THE CASE

1. Is the religious institute of pontifical or diocesan right?
2. Are there any other regions of the institute in a similar situation to the one in South America?
3. Has the need for provincial status come from the members in South America, or is it the decision of the general administration?
4. Can the general administration describe the reason for the many vocations in the area and the potential of these young women to persevere in the institute?
5. Is there evidence that this part of the institute will sustain itself financially without dependence on the generalate?
6. Would the institute have sufficient members qualified to govern the new province, to direct the formation program in that area, and to administer the temporal goods?
7. What has the general administration done to inform the membership as a whole of this development in this particular region of the institute?
8. What has been the general reaction of the membership; are they supportive of the need to advance the region to the provincial level?

Can. 581 To divide an institute into parts, by whatever name they are called, to erect new parts, to join those erected, or to redefine their boundaries belongs to the competent authority of the institute, according to the norm of the constitutions.

COMMENTARY

The canonist should determine the canonical status of the religious institute (c. 589), since a petition for a change in the constitutions must be forwarded to the proper ecclesiastical authority, i.e., CICLSAL or the diocesan bishop of the principal site of the institute (cc. 593, 594, 595 §1). Likewise, it would be important to have a sense of the size of the institute, its parts (houses, regions), their locations, and the ability of the proposed province to sustain itself as a major structure in the institute. It would seem that members sent to a country in South America would need a working knowledge of Spanish or Portuguese and understand to some degree the culture of the people of that country. Another consideration would be the ability of the institute to supply members with training in formation for those seeking admission to the proposed province, since the Church encourages that formation take place within the candidates' culture (*PI* 43, n.2).

An important consideration would be the input of those members in the region. Has the impetus for this change come from them, and do they anticipate this development? What are the apostolic works of the members in the region, and what is the potential for the financial security of the province (cc. 620, 621, 634 §1)? It would also be important to secure the support of the membership of the entire institute for this development in South America. Has sufficient information been accorded the general membership, and how have they reacted favorably to the possibility of a new province?

When the canonist has gathered the above information and recognizes the structural change of the region to a province as beneficial for the institute and the Church, he or she would advise that the norms of the constitutions have to be revised in order to provide for this part. The present constitution is more restrictive than canon 581 of the *Code of Canon Law*. The canonist should recommend that the upcoming ordinary chapter of affairs advise CICLSAL by a two-third vote of the need for the revision of the constitutions and submit interim statutes for the governance of the new province. In this way, the institute could proceed *ad experimentum* with the new province. By the next ordinary chapter, the statutes that have been implemented and perhaps modified should be presented for a two-thirds vote and submitted to CICLSAL for approval and insertion into the constitutions. The bishop of the diocese of the principal site would be the appropriate authority for an institute of diocesan right. It is always helpful to these authorities when both the former and new texts of the law are submitted.

Providing norms for the new structure would afford the institute the opportunity of looking at the entire government structure of the institute. Is this new province the only province; should allowance be made for the erection of other provinces? Are the members satisfied that the principle of subsidiarity is employed in the constitutions? In other words, the government structure of the institute should be thoroughly reviewed at this time.

The canonist should assist in formulating the proposal for the general chapter. He or she should have the chapter body study canon 581 and note the phrase "competent authority." This phrase could mean the superior general with the consent of the council or the general chapter. However, it seems more feasible that the general superior with the consent of the council divides, erects, suppresses, joins, and/or redefines parts of the institute, rather than waiting until a general chapter is convoked for what may be a most practical decision. Canon 581 allows the competent authority to structure the necessary parts of the institute (provinces, regions, districts, houses) according to the institute's need for communal life and service to the particular churches. The constitutions should then describe the parts of the institute in greater detail, i.e., the province, the office of provincial superior, and the responsibilities of the provincial council. What are the decisions the provincial superior will make in accord with canon law?

When an affirmative reply is received for the superior general to erect the province and provide statutes *ad experimentum* to be eventually included in the constitutions, the general superior should notify the diocesan bishop since he either has or will give written consent for the establishment of the house where the provincial house will be located (c. 609 §1). Then the general superior erects the province in keeping with canon 581 and the interim statutes approved *ad experimentum* by CICLSAL. With the establishment of the province, it becomes a public juridic person by the law itself in accord with canon 634.

HELPFUL REFERENCES

- Holland, Sharon. "Internal Governance in Consecrated Life." *CLSA Proceedings* 45 (October 10-13, 1983) 37-48.

- McDermott, Rose. "External and Internal Reconfiguration of Religious Institutes (Canons 582 and 581 CIC)." *Commentarium Pro Religiosis et Missionariis* 86/I-II: 57-81.

- Torres, Jesus. "Ecclesiastical Approval of Constitutions - Meaning and Scope." *Consecrated Life* 9/1 (1984) 120-130.

PETITION TO ROME FOR CHANGE IN CONSTITUTIONS

I, _____, General Superior of the _____, an institute of pontifical right whose generalate is located in _____ diocese, petition for a change in paragraph _____ of our Constitutions. The general chapter which met this past month approved the change by a two-third vote. The revisions of paragraph _____ reads:

> That the general superior with the consent of the council divide the institute into parts, erect new parts, join those erected, and redefine the institute's boundaries according to the norms of the constitutions.

This norm agrees more closely with the provision for institutes of consecrated life as provided in canon 581 of the *Code of Canon Law*.

I also submit the necessary changes in our proper law (*Constitutions* and *Directory*) describing the erection of the province, the office of the provincial superior, her election and authority, as well as the election and responsibilities of the four councilors, and the choice of the treasurer and secretary assisting the provincial council.

Thank you, _____, for your tireless service to institutes of consecrated life and societies of apostolic life.

Gratefully yours,

_____
General Superior

Date:_____

REPLY OF CONGREGATION FOR CONSECRATED LIFE
TO SUPERIOR GENERAL

Prot. n._____

Dear Sister_____,

This Congregation for Institutes of Consecrated Life and Societies of Apostolic Life has received your letter requesting the approval of a change in the Constitutions of _____, as proposed by the 1996 General Chapter.

With this letter, we approve the requested revision of article _____ so that it provides for the General Superior with the consent of the Council to erect, divide, join and suppress parts of the Institute in accord with canon 581.

In view of this approval, you with your Council may proceed in reference to the _____ region, making the necessary provisions.

We note your intent to study your proper law during this term of office for changes which may be required, and your intent that these be brought to the Chapter in 2000. Know that we are ready to be of any possible assistance in this work.

With prayer for God's blessings and with personal best wishes, I remain.

Yours sincerely in Christ,

_____
/s/ Prefect

_____
/s/ Undersecretary

Case 4

Constituted Houses and Erected Houses of a Religious Institute
Canons 581, 608 and 609

Case

A major superior of a religious institute calls to inform the vicar for religious that the institute intends to purchase a house in the archdiocese as a place of rest and revitalization for the sisters returning from their missionary apostolate after six or more years. Because of the nature of the institute and its missionary works, the sisters do not plan to engage in any apostolate in the particular church. The institute has chosen the archdiocese for the site of this temporary residence for their sisters because of the hospitals, retreat centers, and Catholic colleges and universities where the religious can receive the necessary health care and spiritual renewal for their continued work in the missions. The major superior asks what are the canonical requirements necessary when informing the archbishop of this decision to purchase a house. What advice should the vicar for religious give this major superior?

QUESTIONS PERTINENT TO THE CASE

1. Is the institute of pontifical or diocesan right; where are the generalate and provincialate located?
2. Is the institute an international religious institute; how many members and provinces are there and where are they located?
3. Is this the first house to be constituted or erected in the archdiocese?
4. How did the major superior learn of the archdiocese and its advantages of health care and educational facilities?
5. Is missionary activity the sole proper work of the institute?
6. Has the major superior spoken initially with the archbishop regarding this decision?
7. Has she spoken to the pastor of the parish wherein the house to be purchased is located?

THE LAW

Can. 608 A religious community must live in a legitimately established house under the authority of a superior designated according to the norm of law. Each house is to have at least an oratory in which the Eucharist is to be celebrated and reserved so that it is truly the center of the community.

Can. 609 §1. The erection of houses takes place with consideration for their advantage to the Church and the institute and with suitable safeguards for those things which are required to carry out properly the religious life of the members according to the proper purposes and spirit of the institute.

§2. No house is to be erected unless it can be judged prudently that the needs of the members will be provided for suitably.

Canon 611 The consent of the diocesan bishop to erect a religious house of any institute entails the right:

1° to lead a life according to the character and proper purposes of the institute;

2° to exercise the works proper to the institute according to the norm of law and without prejudice to the conditions attached to the consent;

3° for clerical institutes to have a church, without prejudice to the prescript of can. 1215, §3 and to perform sacred ministries, after the requirements of the law have been observed.

COMMENTARY

As the vicar for religious engages the major superior in dialogue, his inquiries should enable him to determine the canonical status of the institute, its vitality and number of its members, its missionary activities, its presence in other dioceses, the location of its generalate and provincialate(s), and the any other reasons why this particular church was chosen apart from proximity to health care and educational institutions. In other words, the vicar for religious is determining the stability of the institute. If the religious institute has already constituted or erected houses in the archdiocese, the vicar for religious would already have much of this information. However, given the nature and end of the institute (missionary activity), it would seem that it would not have a presence in the archdiocese until this venture.

Once the canonical status and stability of the religious institute have been determined, the vicar for religious should explain to the major superior the difference between a "constituted" house and an "erected" house of a religious institute. All houses of religious can be described as in canon 608 above: a house containing a community of men or women religious subject to the authority of a superior designated in accord with the norms of law, with an oratory in which the Eucharist is celebrated and reserved as the center of the community.

Some houses are simply constituted, since there is no intent for them to have the permanence of a generalate, a provincialate, or a large house to which a school or some other proper work of the institute is attached as a proper work of the institute. There are many such houses of religious, particularly those housing religious entrusted with works of the diocese: parish convents, high school faculty houses; small residences where nurses and health care religious reside while serving in a hospital or retirement facility. The competent authority in the proper law of the institute constitutes such a house (c. 581), and certainly the diocesan bishop of the particular church should be advised. Often he is aware of the constituted houses, for it is he who has requested and entrusted the service of the religious in the schools, nursing facilities, and/or social service institutions of the diocese. Many times an oratory is already present in a parish convent or faculty house, but if this is not so, and the religious institute in question is not clerical, the local ordinary would visit the house to determine the suitability of the place for divine worship (c. 1223).

Other houses are canonically erected in accord with canon 609, after having obtained the prior written permission of the diocesan bishop. Since these houses will have permanence in the diocese and offer apostolic service, it is important for the diocesan bishop before giving written consent to investigate carefully the religious institute seeking such permanence in the particular church as far as: 1) its contribution or usefulness to the diocese, 2) the stability of the institute regarding membership, 3) its financial resources and provision for members assigned to the house, and 4) the institute's ability to fulfill the witness and service promised to the particular church for an extended period of time (c. 609). Likewise, the diocesan bishop has to clarify with the major superior the apostolic work agreed on, and the need of the competent authority of the institute to seek his permission if there is a decision to alter the apostolic work or to offer additional works in the particular church (c. 612).

Since this particular religious institute does not plan to serve the archdiocese in any way, the house may be either simply constituted by the competent authority or canonically erected with the prior written consent of the diocesan bishop (c. 609 §1). Sometimes, however, proper law determines the number of delegates for general or provincial chapters based on whether a house is constituted or erected. Also, a canonically erected house, a juridic person in law, is capable of acquiring, possessing, administering, and alienating temporal goods unless the capacity is excluded or restricted by the constitutions of the institute (c. 634 §1).

The vicar for religious should offer these considerations to the major superior and assist her when the decision is reached. He should inform the diocesan bishop as to the decision of the competent authority with regard to the desired canonical status of the house. Likewise, he should suggest that the superior make an appointment with the pastor of the parish in which the house will be located. Good mutual religious would warrant inviting him to dinner when the new community gathers. Since the sisters anticipate having the Blessed Sacrament, there are times when the Eucharist is to be celebrated and hosts changed (c. 934 §2). The pastor of the parish would be most helpful to the religious in these circumstances.

HELPFUL REFERENCES

- Hill, Richard, S.J. "A House is more than a Home." *Review for Religious* 48 (1989) 136-141.

- Holland, Sharon, I.H.M. "'Religious House' according to Canon 608." *The Jurist* 50 (1990) 524-552.

- McDonough, Elizabeth. "Religious Houses - Acquisition of Rights." *CLSA Proceedings* 46 (1884) 149-160.

- _____ "Regarding Small Communities." *Consecrated Life* (1975) 141-145.

Case 5

The Merger or Union of an Institute of Consecrated Life
Canon 582

Case

A *small religious congregation having approximately thirty-eight members, has had no vocations for the past fifteen years. During the past five years the membership has studied other congregations having a similar spirit and end with the intention of uniting with another or united with other small institutes. The leadership of the institute has sought advice from various sources as to the procedure for such a venture.*

QUESTIONS PERTINENT TO THE CASE

1. Is the congregation of pontifical or diocesan right?
2. Is it in close proximity to any of the other congregations having the same spirit and end?
3. Has the leadership addressed this possibility with the membership or is it still at the level of the major superior and council?
4. If the membership has been consulted, what are their feelings and thoughts regarding the possibility of a merger or union?
5. What are the ages of the thirty-eight religious; are many still active; what are the apostolates in which they serve; what is the institute's financial condition?
6. Has the alternative of accepting gradual extinction been raised?
7. From what sources did the leadership seek advice; and what was the advice given?
8. Has the major superior discussed this with the diocesan bishop of the principal site of the institute; what are his thoughts regarding the merger or union of the institute?
9. Has a canonist been consulted; did the canonist review the steps in a merger and union?
10. Are the members aware that ecclesiastical authority encourages mergers and unions to continue the life and mission of the institute?

27

Can. 582 Mergers and unions of institutes of consecrated life are reserved to the Apostolic See only; confederations and federations are also reserved to it.

COMMENTARY

In such a procedure, that will undoubtedly have implications for each and every member of the institute, it would be well to involve all of the members from the beginning. This can be done through general assemblies or written communication advising the members of the three possibilities: 1) gradual extinction, 2) merging with another institute, or 3) uniting with one or more institutes. Ecclesiastical authorities favor a merger or union encouraging institutes with a small number of members to seek out other institutes sharing the same spirit and ends (*PC* 19 and *ES* II:40-41). It would be important, too, to keep the diocesan bishop of the site of the generalate informed, as his *nihil obstat* is required by CICLSAL. This is not so much his consent, as his statement that he has no problem or concern with the decision of the institute to merge or unite with other institutes..

Since the institute is so small, it would seem that assemblies would be more effective in enabling the religious to ask questions and to resolve anxieties they may be experiencing due to this significant event in their lives. There should be ample spiritual, emotional, and canonical preparation of the members as they study the three options presented of eventual extinction, merging with an institute or uniting with two or more institutes sharing the same nature, spirit, and ends. A realistic factor may be the ages of the thirty-eight members, and this should sensitively and clearly be explained. If the members are well advanced in years, it may be difficult to find another institute or institutes willing to risk a merger or union, since the leadership of those institutes may be concerned that they cannot meet the needs of more retired members than it already has.

After all has been explained, it would be well to take a preliminary consultative vote to see how each member views the various options. The process should not be hurried; a committee or the administration should undertake a thorough study of institutes having a like nature, spirit, and end. It would be important from the beginning to petition the institute or institutes that seem most attractive to see if there is a possible interest in a merger or union. It would be disastrous to present such possibilities to the membership, building up their hopes, only to discover that the institute or institutes of choice are not open such an undertaking.

Time is also needed by the administration and members of the institute or institutes interested in the proposal of the small institute. The administration would need to weigh the pros and cons, and advise the members of this possibility. This congregation, too, should take a preliminary vote to see the thinking of each member regarding the possibility. A merger or union may bring financial liability to a congregation; at other times, it could bring financial security, depending on the financial situation and personnel resources of the merging community. The institute or institutes interested, whether of pontifical or diocesan right, should keep the diocesan bishops of the sites of their generalates informed, since his *nihil obstat* is likewise required.

Once the receiving institute or institutes have agreed to the merger, it would be important for members of the institutes to meet with each other in spiritual and social settings. In some instances, they may already know one another through sharing in apostolic works. Gatherings of such a nature can be beneficial in helping the religious familiarize themselves with one another and assuaging the fears of those hesitant or suspicious of such a step. In this latter case, it is important to impress on the religious the freedom that the institute and each member has to make a decision. An individual member deciding against a merger or union is free to seek a transfer to another institute or to petition for an indult of departure. However, the Church favors mergers and unions for small institutes in order to perpetuate their spiritual gift and contribution to the life and holiness of the Church.

While the canonical procedures should be fully explained to the members in the interested institutes, it should not be undertaken until the study, mutual agreement of the institutes, and the willingness of the members is well underway. A canonist called to assist with the procedure should be most sensitive to the fact that one institute or more institutes are about to make a total sacrifice of their identity in order to merge or unite with the life or lives of other institutes. The canonist should do all in his or her power to assure the members of the merging or uniting institutes that they move in the spirit and mind of the Church, that the decision perpetuates life and mission, and that they contribute to the institute or institutes involved in the merger or union as well as to the mission of the Church. All civil laws applicable to the process must be obeyed. The members will welcome the fact that they do not make a new profession, but remain in the same juridical condition in which they are at present.

If the members decide to accept gradual extinction or if they cannot find an institute or institutes with which to merge or unite, a canonist should make clear to them that they must prepare for this event also through careful spiritual and financial planning for the well-being of the members. The institute has fulfilled its part and contributed to the life and mission of the Church. It should be explained that the Spirit's gift of religious life will not be lost to the Church even though some religious institutes will cease to exist. In the meantime, the religious must continue to witness to the Church by the holiness of their lives and their faith in Christ as they enter more deeply into his Paschal Mystery.

HELPFUL REFERENCES

* Blair, Melanie and Jordan Hite. "The Merger and Union of Religious Institutes." *Bulletin on Issues of Religious Law* 3/1 (1987) 1-7.

* Darcy, Catherine, "Restructuring Religious Institutes: A Canonical

Perspective." *Bulletin on Issues of Religious Law* 15 (Fall 1997) 1-12.

- Eichten, Beatrice. "Merger Issues and Ways to Address Them." *Review for Religious* 57 (1988) 394-406.

- Hill, Richard. "Combining Religious Institutes." *Review for Religious* 47 (1988) 141-144.

- Holland, Sharon. "New Institutes, Mergers, and Suppression." *Procedural Handbook for Institutes of Consecrated Life and Societies of Apostolic Life.* Washington, D.C.: Canon Law Society of America, 2001: 41-47.

- McDermott, Rose. "External and Internal Reconfiguration of Religious Institutes (Canons 582 and 581 CIC)." *Commentarium Pro Religiosis et Missionariis* 86/I-II: 57-81.

- Smith, S.C., Rosemary. "Looking to the Future: Alternatives to Consider." *Bulletin on Issues of Religious Law* 18 (Fall 2000) 1-8.

MERGER OF RELIGIOUS INSTITUTES - DOCUMENTS REQUIRED

Institute Requesting the Merger

1. Petition of the Superior General
2. Brief history of the Institute (not more than two pages).
3. List of the members: name, surname, age, date of temporary and perpetual profession, their ministry
4. List of the houses and of the dioceses in which the Religious are living
5. Motives for requesting merger
6. Results of voting (Referendum): in favour and against
7. Intention of those voting against merger of their Institute

Institute Accepting the Merger

1. Letter of Superior General
2. Minutes of the General Chapter or General Council, accepting merger
3. Brief history of the Institute (not more than two pages)
4. Number of: Sisters in perpetual and temporal profession; novices and postulants. Average age of the perpetually professed. Number of the houses and the names of the dioceses in which the Religious are living.

Both Institutes

1. Process toward merger: preparation of the members
2. A preliminary agreement regarding the disposition of temporalities according to the norms of Canon and Civil Law

    "Nihil Obstat" of the diocesan Bishops concerned, if the Institute which is requesting the merger is of diocesan right, or of pontifical right, but spread in a few dioceses.

If possible, please forward to the Cash Office of the Congregation for Institutes of Consecrated Life and Societies of Apostolic Life a deposit equivalent to 300 USA $ on account for the expenses of the entire process.

Vatican, 2001

UNION OF RELIGIOUS INSTITUTES - DOCUMENTS REQUIRED

Document Required from Each Institute

1. Petition of the Superior General to the Holy See to have the institute united with others.
2. Brief history of the institute, including the charism, spirituality and the apostolic activities of the institute (two pages).
3. Statistics: number of the members in perpetual and temporary profession; number of novices postulants; age of the perpetually professed members; number of houses in which the members live and the name of the diocese in which they are established.
4. Motives for requiring the union.
5. Acts of the General Chapter approving the union.
6. Results of the voting made in a referendum: in favor and against. Intention of those voting against regarding their future after the union. Those who intend to transfer to another religious institute should indicate also their intention if they will not be admitted to the new perpetual profession or if they will refuse to make this profession.

Documents Prepared Together

1. Process toward union: experiences made to get to know each other.
2. A preliminary agreement regarding the disposition of temporalities of the institutes, according to the norms of canon and civil law.
3. Title, purpose, spirituality and religious habit of the new institute.
4. Place and diocese of the principal seat of the new institute.
5. Six copies of a draft text of Constitutions, accepted by each institute, read to be examined and approved by the first general chapter. If the new institute will be of pontifical right, the text will be approved by the Holy See; if the new institute will be of diocesan right, the text will be approved by the diocesan bishop of the principal seat of the new institute, taking into consideration the observations made by the Holy See.
   If the institutes concerned intend to examine and aprove this draft in another general chapter, in the meantime, in order to have some provisional norms on whcih the sisters may regulate their consecrated life in the new institute, the following norms are to be sent to the Holy See:
   1) regarding the preparation, convocation and the election of the first general officials;
   2) the various stages of the initial formation;
   3) the general, provincial/regional and local government. The approval of these norms are reserved to the Holy See or to the diocesan bishop of the

principal seat, as indicated above.

6. Indicate the name of any sister of one of the institutes concerned, so that the Holy See may appoint her to prepare and to convoke the first general chapter. If the new institute will be of pontifical right, the same sister will be appointed also to preside over the general chapter until the election of the new superior general. If the new institute will be of diocesan right, the chapter, prepared and convoked by the same sister will be presided over by the diocesan bishop of the principal seat of the new institute until the election of the new superior general.

7. Any particular clauses approved by each institute concerned to be observed for a certain period after the union.

If possible, please forward to the Cash Office of the Congregation for Institutes of Consecrated Life and Societies of Apostolic Life a deposit equivalent to $500, USA dollars, for the expenses of the entire process.

Vatican 2002.

Case 6

The Erection of a Federation of Religious Institutes
Canon 582

Case

Sixteen religious institutes of apostolic life having the same founder and patrimony formed a federation over fifteen years ago in the United States. These institutes support one another in their common spirit and goals through annual assemblies and a newsletter enabling them to share values, ideas, needs, and goals to foster and strengthen the spirit and goals of each congregation. The major superiors of the religious institutes approved Statutes containing organizational structures protecting the autonomy of each institute while providing assistance for all.

With the scarcity of vocations, the major superiors recognized the importance of forming novices in the nature, spirit, and ends of their institutes within the framework of communal life rather than individually. They decided to petition CICLSAL for the status of a public juridic person for the federation in order that, with the consent of the appropriate major superior of each institute, the novices could be formed in the spirit and ideals of their common patrimony in a common canonical novitiate. How was this to be accomplished?

QUESTIONS PERTINENT TO THE CASE

1. During the fifteen years the federation was in existence, were there any previous attempts noted in the files of petitioning for the status of a public juridic person in the Church?
2. What are the contents of the statutes? Do they contain basic elements such as a description of its purpose and objectives, government, and requirements for membership and withdrawal?
3. How did the major superiors of the federation reach this decision? Has there been discussion among them and with the members of their respective institutes about this decision?
4. Has there been a presentation made at one or more of the annual assemblies concerning this consideration to seek canonical status, the reasons for it, the

procedures to obtain public status in the Church?
5. Have the statutes been reviewed by a canonist for accuracy and include any amendments the religious may want prior to approval by CICLSAL?
6. Would the religious want anything else included in the approved statutes besides the right of the federation to erect a canonical novitiate?

THE LAW

> Can. 582 Mergers and unions of institutes of consecrated life are reserved to the Apostolic See only; confederations and federations are also reserved to it.

COMMENTARY

This particular federation of institutes had been active for over fifteen years in the United States, having been organized as early as 1990. Years ago, negotiations began with Rome to constitute it as a public juridic person, but communications broke down with the changes in leadership and the obligations of each of the institutes to revise the proper laws of their institutes towards the end of the Second Vatican Council. Sisters studying the archives recognized the unfinished business and petitioned a canonist for help with the requirements Rome would ask for such status in the Church.

The canonist reviewed the statutes of the federation and made recommendations to clarify and strengthen them. A petition was drawn up for CICLSAL and sent with the amended statutes. A reply to the petition asked for the following:

1. Juridical nature of each institute, whether of diocesan or pontifical right and diocese generalate is located;
2. Membership of each institute, number, average age of members in perpetual and temporary profession, as well as novices and postulants, number of houses and dioceses sisters live and minister;
3. *Nihil obstat* of bishop of diocese where generalate of diocesan right institute is located regarding the institute's membership in the federation;
4. Two copies of the revised statutes taking cognizance of the observations made by the staff at CICLSAL.

The executive coordinator of the federation worked with her staff and the major superiors in revising the statutes in accord with the observations of CICLSAL. Copies of the canonical status of each institute, the diocese of the generalate (#1 above) and the requested statistics of each institute (#2 above) were compiled. The institutes of diocesan right obtained a letter from the respective bishops of the diocese in which their generalates were situated indicating they had no objection to the institutes' membership in the federation.

A second cover letter requesting the status of the federation as a public juridic person in the Church accompanied these documents was submitted to CICLSAL. Within a month, the executive director received the following reply from the undersecretary of that dicastery:

Dear Sister _____,

Enclosed you will find the Decree, concerning the erection of the "U.S. *Federation of the* _____" together with the list of the members of the Federation and approved Statutes.

In the list of the members of the Federation you will note that the number of the Congregations are now 15 not 16, since the religious institute of _____ was merged last year (date) with that of _____ of diocesan right with its generalate in the diocese of _____.

We would like to send our congratulations to all the members of the new Federation, being sure that it will continue to promote particularly the spiritual welfare of all the Sisters.

With God's blessing, I remain,

_____
Undersecretary

HELPFUL RESOURCES

- Rose McDermott, SSJ. "Part III Institutes of Consecrated Life and Societies of Apostolic Life (cc. 573-746)." *New Commentary on the Code of Canon Law* edited by John P. Beal, James A. Coriden, and Thomas J. Green. NY/Mahwah: Paulist Press, 2000:750-751.

REQUEST TO FORM A FEDERATION

Prot. n. _____

Decree

Thirteen religious Institutes and two Provinces of two other religious Institutes of _____ in the United States of America, mentioned in the enclosed list, humbly ask the Apostolic See to establish a Federation, in order to ensure mutual aid and coordination between them.

The Congregation for Institutes of Consecrated Life and Societies of Apostolic Life, having attentively examined the matter, by means of this present Decree establishes the

United States Federation

of _____

Moreover, the same Congregation approves and confirms, *for five years,* the text of the Federal Statutes, written in English, which corresponds to the text kept in its archives.

Anything to the contrary notwithstanding.

Vatican, 13 August, 2000.

_____
Prefect

_____
Secretary

Case 7

The Extinction or Suppression of an Institute of Consecrated Life
Canons 120, 584, 616 §2, §4

Case

A *major superior of a religious institute calls the diocesan bishop to set up an appointment with him and the small community of religious. She advises the bishop's secretary that there are only four members remaining in the institute due to lack of vocations, departures, and deaths. During the past two years, the sisters have prayerfully discerned to make decisions regarding their future. The oldest, an eighty-five year old woman, is ready and willing to enter a nursing home; the two religious in their late forties have communicated with the superior general of a congregation similar to the spirit and goals of the present one and decided to transfer; the sister in her early sixties will petition the diocesan bishop to be admitted to the order of virgins and continue her pastoral work in the diocese. The superior general would like the diocesan bishop to meet with the four religious, give them his blessing, and discuss any canonical requirements resultant from their decisions. What would be some considerations the diocesan bishop should have in mind regarding their decisions as he prepares to meet with them?*

QUESTIONS PERTINENT TO THE CASE

1. Is the religious institute of diocesan or pontifical right?
2. Are there any other members on exclaustration or in another form of temporary separation (e.g., permission to live apart from the institute; transferred, but not yet admitted to perpetual profession in the other institute)?
3. How long has the institute been reduced to four members?
4. Did they ever consider merging with a larger institute of similar nature, spirit, and end?
5. Have they consulted counselors, canonists, or civil lawyers to assist them with this decision?
6. Is each of them comfortable and at peace with the decision to permit the institute to become extinct, as well as with her personal decision?
7. What is their financial condition (movable, immovable properties, other patrimony, free capital)?
8. Does the institute have any sponsored works that need to be addressed?

9. Has the institute any significant outstanding debts?

Can. 120 §1. A juridic person is perpetual by its nature; nevertheless, it is extinguished if it is legitimately suppressed by competent authority or has ceased to act for a hundred years. A private juridic person, furthermore, is extinguished if the association is dissolved according to the norm of its statutes or if, in the judgment of competent authority, the foundation has ceased to exist according to the norm of its statutes.

§2. If even one of the members of a collegial juridic person survives, and the aggregate of persons (*universitas personarum*) has not ceased to exist according to its statutes, that member has the exercise of all the rights of the aggregate (*universitas*).

Can. 584 The suppression of an institute pertains only to the Apostolic See; a decision regarding the temporal goods of the institute is also reserved to the Apostolic See.

Can. 616 §2. The suppression of the only house of an institute belongs to the Holy See, to which the decision regarding the goods in that case is also reserved.

§4. To suppress an autonomous monastery of nuns belongs to the Apostolic See, with due regard to the prescripts of the constitutions concerning the goods.

COMMENTARY

The diocesan bishop is indeed fortunate. While he exerts a vigilance over diocesan institutes (c. 594) and is obligated to foster and promote all institutes of consecrated life (c. 576), he does not interfere in their internal government or discipline (c. 586 §2). The four religious, recognizing their own grave obligation to plan for the future, have through a prayerful and painful discernment process come to a communal and personal decisions regarding their vocations as religious.

It would be important to know if the institute is of diocesan or pontifical right. If the former, they would certainly be obligated to address the bishop of the principal site (generalate) with their decisions. He would assist them in the matters addressed below. If they are of pontifical right, they need to be in contact CICLSAL, since they are immediately subject to that congregation. However, since a supreme moderator of any religious institute consults the diocesan bishop before suppressing a legitimately erected house of the institute (c. 616 §1), it seems appropriate that whether the institute be of diocesan or pontifical right that the general superior consult the diocesan bishop in this very grave matter.

One could reasonably ask why the diocesan bishop or his vicar for religious had not raised the possibility of a union or merger with this institute before the members were reduced to four. Given the small number and the fact they seem resolute in their decisions, raising the possibility of merger or union at this juncture may only cause further anxiety. At this difficult period, the diocesan bishop should be particularly sensitive and kind to these religious. Not only are they facing the possible extinction of their religious institute (c. 120), but they are parting from one another after perhaps many years of communal life in the spirit of their charism. Each of these women faces significant disruption and adjustment in her consecrated life. Likewise, they have served the diocese for years, and that should be acknowledged with sincere gratitude by the bishop.

The norms on suppression and extinction are given above. Ordinarily suppression has a negative connotation, and CICLSAL would only suppress an institute if there were some grave moral crisis, e.g., the failure to live out the patrimony of the institute (c. 578) through serious violations against canon law or the constitutions of the institute. In such a case, an apostolic visitator would be delegated to visit an institute of pontifical right, while the diocesan bishop would visit an institute of diocesan right. The visitator would meet with the general superior, each member of the institute, and the community as a whole in order to determine the disposition of each individual and their life together. A detailed report resulting from the visitation would be sent to the Apostolic See advising for or against the suppression with accommodations for the religious.

In the case presented to the diocesan bishop, the decisions of the four religious would lead to the eventual extinction of the institute. The eighty-four year old sister entering the nursing home will be the one member to continue the institute until her death (c. 120 §2). Even with her death, the institute is not extinguished until after one hundred years. The two sisters transferring to another institute will become members of that institute once they complete the probationary period and are admitted to perpetual profession by the competent authority in that institute (cc. 684-685). The bishop would present the third sister's petition to be admitted to the order of virgins to CICLSAL, since that dicastery processes such a petition similar to a transfer requiring CICLSAL's authorization (c. 604). This would preclude her presenting a request an indult of departure to the diocesan bishop (c. 691) or CICLSAL before the bishop could admit her to the order of virgins. In this latter case, it may be well to inquire if the religious had considered transferring to another religious institute and if she is truly committed to serve the diocese.

It would be prudent for the diocesan bishop to inquire about the temporal goods of the institute and how the religious propose to sell properties and distribute the temporal goods. He may already have a good grasp on their financial condition if they have been faithful in sending him a report in accord with canon law (c. 637). He should remind them of their obligation to obey civil laws in this area and the intentions of benefactors to the institute.

Money from the sale of property and other patrimonial funds should be set aside for each of the religious. The sister entering the nursing home should have funds set aside for her care and needs; likewise, the sister about to make the solemn promise of virginity in the diocese should have money set aside for her departure from the institute (c. 702) and her retirement. If she will be working for the diocese, it would seem she would have compensation comparable to that of the lay persons in ministerial positions and provisions for a pension as a layperson. Hopefully, the institute has invested in Social Security which will assist both her and the sister in the nursing facility. Finally, the two sisters transferring should have some monies set aside for their care while in the process of transfer and in the event one or both decide to depart that institute (c. 702). Some funds should be sent to that religious institute towards its retirement fund . The bishop could have his canonist and a prudent financial advisor assist the religious with these provisions.

When the bishop is satisfied that the religious have met all of their canonical obligations regarding their choices, he should advise the general superior (if it is a pontifical right institute) to give an account to CICLSAL and recommend that the one sister seeking consecrated virginity present her petition to that dicastery in order that he consecrate her a virgin in the diocese. If the institute is of diocesan right, he should advise CICLSAL of the facts of the case, assuring that dicastery of his vigilance over the institute and its four members.. It would seem that CICLSAL may formally suppress the institute with the death of the senior sister, since it would continue even then for a hundred years (c. 120 §1). The same dicastery will appreciate all information and the assistance of the diocesan bishop to the sisters, taking note of the facts in the file of the institute. While the canons leave decisions regarding the temporal goods of the institute to the Apostolic See (cc. 584, 616 §2), it would seem the welfare of the religious would be of primary concern, as well as any outstanding debts, liabilities, the will of founders or donors, acquired rights, and compliance with civil laws (cc. 123, 1257 §1, 1258, 1300).

HELPFUL REFERENCES

- Andrés, D. J. "La supresión de los Institutos religiosos. Estudio canónico de los datos más relevantes." *Commentarium pro Religiosis et Missionariis* 1986: 3-54.

- McDonough, Elizabeth. "Beyond the Liberal Model: *Quo Vadis?*" *Studia Canonica* 1992: 307-341.

The above is an example of a gradual extinction of a religious institute. The following decree is an act of suppression of a monastery when there is no hope for new members. The members of the monastery would be welcomed in monasteries of the same institute or federation.

SAMPLE

DECREE OF SUPPRESSION

Congregatio
Pro Institutis Vitae Consecratae
Et Societatibus Vitae Apostolicae

The Congregation for Institutes of Consecrated Life and Societies of Apostolic Life, because of the declining number of nuns and the difficulty for the aging Community, with this present Decree decides to suppress the Monastery of the _____ of _____ in the Diocese of _____ .

The nuns must move to other Monasteries of the same Order, which will be ready to accept them with the same rights and duties which the Nuns enjoyed in their Monastery.

Pious legacies, if there be any, must be used for the purpose intended by the donor or testator; likewise, the rights of others, if there be any, must be preserved intact insofar as the case demands.

It pertains to the _____ (bishop of the diocese) to execute this Decree and to inform this Congregation of its execution.

All things to the contrary notwithstanding.

Vatican City _____ (date)

_____
Secretary

_____
Undersecretary

Case 8

Approval of Changes in Constitutions
of a Religious Institute of Diocesan Right
Canon 587

Case

The supreme moderator of a religious institute of diocesan right petitions the bishop to approve changes approved by the general chapter for the constitutions. The diocesan bishop asks one of the canonists in the tribunal to review the document and submit his recommendations. What are some salient points the canonist should keep in mind as he attempts to review the proper law of the institute?

QUESTIONS PERTAINING TO THE CASE

1. Does the canonist have both parts of the proper law (the constitutions and the directory or statutes)?
2. Has the proper law been generally acceptable to the full membership of the institute and recommended for approval by a two-third vote of the general chapter?
3. Has the superior general petitioned the bishop of the diocese where the principal seat or generalate of the institute is located?
4. Do the constitutions describe accurately the nature, spirit, character, and purpose of the religious institute?
5. Do the constitutions reflect the spirit of the institute and the vocation of the members in norms that are both spiritual and juridic?
6. Are there appropriate chapters in the constitutions describing essential norms pertaining to: governance, temporal goods, admission, formation, incorporation, the sacred bonds, community life, apostolate, and separation from the institute?
7. Does the directory or statutory section of the proper law contain additional norms that are not constitutive, as well as norms that complement the constitutions?
8. In the canonist's opinion does the proper law of the institute serve as an exhortatory and pedagogic document?
9. Is the proper law supplemented by manuals on governance, formation, and/or

temporalities?

10. Does the proper law contain unnecessary or superfluous norms that can easily be deleted from the text?

The Law

Can. 587 §1. To protect more faithfully the proper vocation and identity of each institute, the fundamental code or constitutions of every institute must contain, besides those things which are to be observed as stated in can. 578, fundamental norms regarding governance of the institute, the discipline of members, incorporation and formation of members, and the proper object of the sacred bonds.

§2. A code of this type is approved by competent authority of the Church and can be changed only with its consent.

§3. In this code spiritual and juridic elements are to be joined together suitably; nevertheless, norms are not to be multiplied without necessity.

§4. Other norms established by competent authority of an institute are to be collected suitably in other codes and, moreover, can be reviewed appropriately and adapted according to the needs of places and times.

Can. 594 Without prejudice to can. 586, an institute of diocesan right remains under the special care of the diocesan bishop.

Can. 595 §1. It is for the bishop of the principal seat to approve the constitutions and confirm changes legitimately introduced into them, without prejudice to those things which the Apostolic See has taken in hand, and also to treat affairs of greater importance affecting the whole institute which exceed the power of internal authority, after he has consulted the other diocesan bishops, however, if the institute has spread to several dioceses.

§2. A diocesan bishop can grant dispensations from the constitutions in particular cases.

Commentary

Reviewing and recommending for approval the constitutions of a religious institute of diocesan right is an extremely important and delicate matter both for the particular church and the diocesan right institute. The constitutions protect the patrimony and identity of the institute and describe its nature, purpose, spirit and character as well as its sound traditions. The document contains fundamental norms on governance, discipline of members, incorporation and formation, and the object of the sacred bonds (cc. 578, 587). The constitutions serve as a practical instrument which exhorts members to fidelity and instructs those unfamiliar with the institute. Before the canonist begins working on the document, it would be important for him or her to have both parts (constitutions and directory or statutes). His work will be made considerably easier if the changes are highlighted or italicized. While the diocesan bishop is obliged to approve only the constitutions or changes in it (c. 587 §2), it may be helpful to study the directory or statutes (secondary code) to see if they contain essential elements that should be included in the proper law of the institute (c. 587 §4).

The canonist would be advised to keep the 1983 *Code of Canon Law* open for reference during his review of the proper law. Book II, Part III, Section I on general norms and the norms on religious institutes contain canons of a universal nature that should be included in the constitutive law of religious institutes. For example, a description of the patrimony of the institute (c. 578) and the essential elements of the evangelical counsels of chastity (c. 599), poverty (c. 600) and obedience (c. 601). The norms in the constitutive law reflect these essentials of the vows, while the norms in the directory or statute would contain supplementary norms. This can be seen in canon 600 regarding the vow of poverty. While the constitutions would include the obligation of the act of cession (c. 668 §1), the more detailed obligations of the vow of poverty according to the customs of the institute would be included in the directory or statutes of the institute.

If the canonist has been working with members of the institute in the formulation of the proper law, he or she may suggest that norms in the secondary code (directory or statutes) be correlated with the corresponding canon in the constitutive law. This can be done in various ways. For example, the constitutive norm can be typed in italics followed by the corresponding directive or directives in script. Or the constitutions can be typed completely in section one of the text with numbered paragraphs. The directory would contain sub-paragraphs complementing the numbered paragraphs of the constitutions. Another practical measure is to place the pages in a loose-leaf binder rather than having the documents bound. If changes are made and approved in either of the sections (constitutions or directory). they can be more easily inserted into a binder.

Some universal norms in Book II, Part III are of the utmost importance because they protect fundamental rights of both the institute and the members. Such would be true, for example, of the procedural norms on separation from the institute (cc. 684-704). These canons are either copied directly into the constitutions of the institute or a statement is made in the chapter on separation that the procedures for transfer, exclaustration, departure, and dismissal are carried out "in accord with canon law." These norms and others similar to them are interpreted strictly and followed with great precision by ecclesiastical authorities for the validity of acts of separation be they voluntary or involuntary.

Other norms directly (cc. 598 §1, 609 §1) or indirectly (c. 578) refer to the constitutions or fundamental code of the various institutes. Their contents should be included in the constitutive section of the proper law of the religious institute. Likewise, some of the canons in Book II, Part III of the code simply refer to the *ius proprium* or proper law of the institute (cc. 573 §2, 627 §2). Since the more generic term, proper law is used, the canonist understands that the norms can be placed in either the constitutions or the directory as decided by the institute. For example, it would seem that the procedure for valid acts of extraordinary administration (c. 638 §1) should be placed in the constitutions, whereas acts of ordinary administration can be placed in the constitutions or directory of the institute (c. 638 §2).

A general principle of law is that the proper law can be more restrictive than universal law, but it cannot be less restrictive than the universal law. For example, if the universal law requires the consent of the council for certain acts (e.g., c. 638 §3), the proper law must require the consent of the council. However, if the universal law requires the advice of the council (e.g., c. 697), the proper law can require the consent of the council. Those composing the proper law of the institute would do well to follow the norms of the code. The canons reflect years of accumulated wisdom on the part of experts. If too many restrictive norms are placed in the constitutions, or if items that could well be placed in the directory or statutes are written into the constitutions, the proper authorities of the institute will have to seek dispensations from them in carrying on their administrative responsibilities.

Another important consideration is that subsequent changes made in the document be accepted by the members of the institute as reflected by a two-thirds vote of the general chapter. Since all of the members profess to live their lives in accord with the law of the institute (c. 654), it would seem that the entire membership should have been consulted through a referendum prior to the convocation of the general chapter (cc. 115 §2, 119 3°). Only the changes submitted by the chapter need to be presented to the diocesan bishop, since the rest of the constitutions have already been approved.

HELPFUL REFERENCES

- Hite, Jordan, T.O.R. "Appendix 2 Canons That Refer to the Constitutions and Proper Law of Institutes of Consecrated Life and Societies of Apostolic Life." *Religious Institutes Secular Institutes Societies of Apostolic Life A Handbook on Canons 573-746* edited by Jordan Hite, T.O.R., Sharon Holland, I.H.M., and Daniel Word, O.S.B. Collegeville: The Liturgical Press, 1985.

- McDonough, Elizabeth. "Constitutions." *Review for Religious* (1991) 456-460.

- O'Reilly, Michael A. "The Proper Law of Institutes of Religious Life and of Societies of Apostolic Life." *Unico Ecclesiae Servitio.* Edited by M. Theriault and J. Thorn. Ottawa: St. Paul University Press, 1991: 287-306.

- Sundara, Raj J. "The Juridical nature of the Religious Constitutions in the Law of the Church." *Commentarium pro Religiosis et Missionariis* (1991) 211-260.

- Thomas, Barbara L. "Constitutions and Canon Law." *The Way Supplement* (1984) 47-60.

48

Case 9

Restrictions on the Authority of a Diocesan Bishop
for an Institute of Diocesan Right
Canon 595 §1

Case

*A student states in class that he understands the authority of the diocesan
bishop of the principal seat to confirm changes legitimately introduced into the
constitutions of an institute of diocesan right as described in canon 595 §1.
However, he does not know what kind of changes in the constitutions that would be
taken in hand by the Apostolic See and would appreciate some examples of that
kind.*

THE LAW

> Can. 595 §1. It is for the bishop of the principal seat to approve the
> constitutions and confirm changes legitimately introduced into them,
> without prejudice to those things which the Apostolic See has taken in hand,
> and also to treat affairs of greater importance affecting the whole institute
> which exceed the power of internal authority, after he has consulted the
> other diocesan bishops, however, if the institute has spread to several
> dioceses.

COMMENTARY

The diocesan bishop of the principal seat of an institute of diocesan right can
approve constitutions and confirm changes in them that are not contrary to the
universal law of the Church in accord with the nature, character, spirit, and end of
the institute as a public juridic person in the Church. Likewise, he can approve
changes legitimately introduced. Again, the changes cannot be contrary to the
universal law. If the members of the institute did approve something in their
general chapter contrary to the universal law or what contrary to the nature,
purpose, and end presented at their approval, they would be required to seek
permission or obtain a dispensation from CICLSAL. This dispensation would not

seem to be given easily, since the essential elements of the nature, purpose, and goals of the institute are constituent to the institution.

Two examples could be given of such changes reserved to the Apostolic See. The first change was petitioned by the religious institute; the second change was introduced by the decree *Perfectae Caritatis* concerning the vow of poverty in religious congregations of simple vows.

The Mercedarians are a religious institute founded in Spain in 1220 by St. Peter Nolasco and dedicated to Our Lady of Mercy. The members of that Crusader military order vowed to accept captivity in exchange for Christians captured by the Turks during the time of the Crusades. This was the design of their founder and their purpose at that particular time in the history of the Church. Gradually, the need for such a vow and commitment was no longer necessary, and the clerical institute petitioned the Apostolic See that the purpose of their institute would address the needs of contemporary times through an apostolate of mercy to the sick and imprisoned. This end or goal both conformed to their dedication to Our Lady of Mercy and addressed the needs of God's people in contemporary society.

Since the acceptance of captivity for the release of a prisoner was the design of the founder and the purpose of the religious institute because of the charism or spirit of mercy, that apostolate constituted the patrimony of the institute (cc. 578, 587 §1). To address the needs of contemporary times required a change not so much in the nature or spirit of the institute, but in the designs of the founder who wanted the institute to address the plight of these Christian prisoners. Such a constitutive change reflective of the end or goal of the institute was reserved to the Apostolic See.

Another example would be the change in the provision for the vow of poverty in an institute of simple profession. Canon 581 of the 1917 *Code of Canon Law* prohibited a religious who had professed simple vows from renouncing his or her property with the exception of those about to make solemn profession. The decree on religious life, *Perfectae Caritatis* in paragraph 13 permits religious congregations (institutes with simple vows) to provide in their constitutions that members can renounce their inheritances, both those which they have already acquired and those acquired in the future. *Ecclesiae Sanctae* II:24 permitted the general chapters of the institutes of simple vows to decide on this issue. This was a significant change in the provisions of the vow of poverty for those institutes with simple vows, and the change introduced by the conciliar decree was provided for in canon 668 §4 of the *Code of Canon Law*. This was a change in the universal law for religious congregations and could not have been introduced or approved by diocesan bishops prior to the provision by the conciliar decree of the council.

A diocesan bishop could not approve a change in constitutions that would be contrary to what is provided in the universal law. Nor could a diocesan bishop change or give approval for a change in the patrimony of an institute, e.g., it nature, spirit, or purpose. Such changes are left to the supreme authority in the Church (the pope or an ecumenical council).

- Sharon Holland, IHM. "Section I:Institutes of Consecrated Life (cc. 573-730)." *The Code of Canon Law A Text and Commentary* edited by James A. Coriden, Thomas J. Green, and Donald E. Heintschel. New York/Mahwah: Paulist Press, 1985:463.

- Rose McDermott, SSJ. "Part III Institutes of Consecrated Life and Societies of Apostolic Life (cc. 573-746)." *New Commentary on the Code of Canon Law* edited by John P. Beal, James A. Coriden, and Thomas J. Green. New York/Mahwah: Paulist Press, 2000:751.

Case 10

The Eremitical Life - A Renewed Form of Consecrated Life
Canon 603

Case

A gentleman in his mid-forties writes to the diocesan bishop. The man advises the bishop that he would like to become a hermit in the diocese. He had been in a religious institute, but finds the eremitical lifestyle more attractive. The bishop asks his canonical advisor to interview the man and give a recommendation. What are some concerns the canonist should have as he or she prepares to meet with the gentleman?

QUESTIONS PERTINENT TO THE CASE

1. Why is the gentleman choosing this particular diocese; does he live in the diocese?
2. How long had the gentleman been in religious life; why did he leave?
3. What was the name of the institute; has he an indult of departure or a decree of dismissal if he had been in perpetual profession?
4. Where was the man born, what of the practice of his faith, in what parish is he presently registered or residing?
5. How long has the gentlemen been out of religious life, and what has he been doing?
6. What does he understand about the eremitical life; does he realize the demands of this rather challenging way of life?
7. Has he discussed this vocation or way of life with a spiritual director or counselor?
8. Does he have any formal training in theology or spirituality; did he take courses in theology or spirituality in the religious institute?
9. How does he plan to provide for his financial needs: room and board, health care, retirement?
10. What are his expectations of the diocese regarding his vocation?
11. Does he envision his vocation as lived alone, or does he see it possibly attracting others to the eremitical life in company with him?

Can. 603 §1. In addition to institutes of consecrated life, the Church recognizes the eremitic or anchoritic life by which the Christian faithful devote their life to the praise of God and the salvation of the world through a stricter withdrawal from the world, the silence of solitude, and assiduous prayer and penance.

§2. A hermit is recognized by law as one dedicated to God in consecrated life if he or she publicly professes in the hands of the diocesan bishop the three evangelical counsels, confirmed by vow or other sacred bond, and observes a proper program of living under his direction.

COMMENTARY

Perhaps the two canons in the section on consecrated life that place great responsibility on the diocesan bishop since the Second Vatican Council are canons 603 and 604. While the eremtical life is a form of consecrated life, and the order of virgins *resembles (accedit)* consecrated life (virgins make a solemn promise of virginity), these vocations are lived by individuals not joined to institutes which are approved as public juridic persons in the Church (religious institutes, secular institutes, and societies of apostolic life). Therefore, it is important from the start, that the bishop understands these men and women will be living on their own and providing for themselves. While the diocese has no financial responsibility towards them, it may well have moral responsibility if the diocesan bishop approves the person as living a form of consecrated life in his diocese.

It would be important to understand the length of time this man has resided in the diocese. Has he lived there all of his life, or has he been refused by diocesan bishops in other dioceses and is "shopping" for a benevolent bishop? An interesting fact is that he has been in religious life. The canonist should carefully question the man as to the name of the religious institute, the time spent in it, his status at departure (postulant, novice, temporary professed, perpetually professed) the reason for his voluntary or involuntary separation from it. Likewise, if he had been in perpetual profession, he should have an indult of departure or a decree of dismissal from the institute. The name of the institute would be important, since the diocesan bishop would consult the major superior prior to admitting this man to the eremitical life (see c. 645 §2 by analogy). It would be important to know the reasons for departure or dismissal, as well as the general behavior of the man while in the religious institute.

Next a general understanding of the early background of the man would be important. Where was he born, how long a Catholic, how has he practiced his faith, how old was he when he entered religious life, was he ever married? What is his general health, his present occupation, his attitude towards others and family and communal life? Has he a spiritual director, is he involved in his parish and known by his pastor?

To live the eremitical life would seem to involve some understanding of the life and the evangelical counsels. While it is true the man has been in religious life and perhaps (if professed in the institute) lived the counsels. But it will be a radically different experience to live them apart from a religious institutes with its norms, guidelines, and communal support for living the counsels. Religious institutes provide all of the necessities needed for their members to carry out their vocations (c. 670), but the person living an eremitical lifestyle will have to provide for himself or herself.

The educational background of the man would be important in determining his fitness for the life. Has he had any formal or informal training in theology or spirituality? Does he understand the canonical requirements of the life as described in c. 603 §2? Has he considered or written a program of life to be submitted to the diocesan bishop regarding the way he will live out his vocation (c. 603 §2)? Has he considered having others join him in the eremitical life with the intention of eventually petitioning for the status of a religious institute (c. 579)?

Finally, it is important to see what the gentleman's expectations of the diocese are. Does he think that it will provide for him financially (property, stipend, health care, retirement) as it does for secular clergy? Where is his residence at present, and does he plan to convert it into a hermitage? How will he sustain himself as a hermit; what are his gifts that could be used to support this vocation? How does he plan to provide for health benefits and retirement? It would be important to indicate at this time that the diocesan bishop, if willing to accept him as a hermit in the diocese, would require him to sign a waiver acknowledging that the diocese is in no way responsible for him nor his family financially.

Many bishops hesitate to accept such persons, men or women, because they do not possess competent persons in their diocese educated in the monastic life that could assist these persons through a formative program. Even if they have such persons, they are probably already overworked and could ill afford to give one person the time and expertise needed to be formed in the eremitical vocation. It would seem the canons on formation in religious life would be helpful, and a bishop should not receive the public profession of a hermit unless there has been a period of formation in accord with the proper program of living agreed on by the diocesan bishop and the candidate in accord with canon 603 §2.

HELPFUL REFERENCES

- Andrés, D. J., "Proyecto de Estatutos diocesanos para los Ermitaños de una Iglesia particular. Comentario aplicativo al can. 603 del Código." *Commentarium pro Religiosis Missionariis* (1986) 185-248.

- Egan, Scholatica. "The Hermits Are Back." *Religious Life Review* 36/182 (Jan./Feb. 1997) 35-38.

- Holland, Sharon. "From the Silence of Solitude." *Informationes* 28/2 (2002) 100-110.

- MacDonald, Helen. "Hermits: The Juridical Implications of Canon 603." *Studia Canonica* 26 (1992) 163-189.

- McDermott, Rose. "Recent Developments in Consecrated Life." *Bulletin on Issues of Religious Law* vol. 9 (Fall 1993) 1-9.

- McDonough, Elizabeth. "Hermits and Virgins." *Review for Religious* (1992) 303-308.

Case 11

The Order of Virgins and Consecration by the Diocesan Bishop
Canon 604

Case
*A woman has written to the diocesan bishop requesting to be consecrated a
virgin. The bishop asks one of the canonists to interview the woman and make a
recommendation to him. What are some considerations the canonist should keep
in mind as he or she prepares for the interview?*

QUESTIONS PERTINENT TO THE CASE

1. Is the woman a member of the diocese?
2. How old is she, and what is her canonical status?
3. Was she or is she married, an impediment which preclude consecrated virginity.
4. Is she a professed religious whose institute has the tradition of incorporating the
   rite of virginity within the profession ceremony?
5. Was she ever a candidate, novice or professed member in a religious institute;
   if she was incorporated into an institute, does she have an indult of departure or
   decree of dismissal? Why did she depart or why was she dismissed from the
   institute?
6. How does she practice her Catholic faith; does she have a spiritual director with
   whom she   has discussed this desire; did she discuss this vocation with her
   pastor?
7. Has she ever engaged in public or flagrant violation of chastity?
8. How did she come to the knowledge of this form of consecrated life?
9. What is her general understanding of consecrated virginity; does she understand
   its obligations?
10. How does she provide for her financial security; does she realize that the
    diocese is not obliged to support her as a consecrated virgin?
11. How does she intend to serve the Church as a consecrated virgin?

THE LAW

> Can. 604 §1. Similar to these forms of consecrated life is the order of
> virgins who, expressing the holy resolution of following Christ more
> closely, are consecrated to God by the diocesan bishop according to the

approved liturgical rite, are mystically betrothed to Christ, the Son of God, and are dedicated to the service of the Church.

§2. In order to observe their own resolution more faithfully and to perform by mutual assistance service to the Church in harmony with their proper state, virgins can be associated together.

COMMENTARY

For any vocation in the Catholic Church, the canonical status of the person must be clearly delineated so as to determine the suitability and freedom of the person to undertake the particular calling. The woman aspiring to be a consecrated virgin should be a baptized Catholic in the Latin church and a member of the diocese over which the bishop she petitions has pastoral care. Likewise, she should have never married and be free from any impediments that would preclude the bishop's consecrating her.

Age would seem to be important, since the woman should have sufficient maturity and experience to understand the vocation to a life of virginity. The canonist should carefully inquire as to her reception of the sacraments of initiation, her practice of the faith and a chaste life, her registration or worship in a parish community, and the recommendation of her parish priest. The rite states that consecrated virginity is for those "that have never married nor lived in public or flagrant violation of chastity." So it would seem that a woman who may have lost her virginity through an indiscreet act as a teenager, is contrite and has lived chastely for a significant period of time would not be barred from this consecration. In this case the woman should discuss this situation with her spiritual director or her confessor. Since her indiscretion was not public nor flagrant, the diocesan bishop's decision to admit her to the order of virgins would not seem to cause *admiratio* on the part of the Christian faithful.

It would be important to learn how the woman came to the knowledge of this particular vocation and its implications and obligations. Finally, the canonist should discreetly inquire as to the woman's financial security, and her understanding that the diocese is not obligated to support a woman in this vocation. If the woman has a profession, she should consider ways that she could offer some service to the Church, e.g., catechetical instruction, special minister of the Eucharist, participation in the choir or cantor, service on the parish pastoral or finance council.

Depending on the age and spiritual maturity of the woman, a period of formation in this particular vocation would be important. The diocesan bishop could place her under the care of a canonist, vocation director, or the vicar for religious, as she lives in the spirit of this vocation. During this period of time, she should have careful instruction in the life of virginity, be encouraged to read articles, study the rite of consecration, and be docile to her spiritual director and the person entrusted with her formation. The length of this formative period would depend on her spiritual maturity and the time she had already been living this lifestyle.

In accord with canon 604 §1, the diocesan bishop has the authority to consecrate the woman to God in a life of virginity. If he cannot perform the liturgical rite, he should delegate another bishop to do so, since there is an explicit relationship of the consecrated virgin with the diocesan bishop and particular church. It would be wise prior to the consecration that the woman understand the diocese is under no obligation to support her or members of her family. Civil lawyers have recommended that a waiver be signed by the woman on the day of consecration indicating her understanding that the diocese is not liable for her financial security. The bishop or canonist should be certain that the woman has a position and means to support herself; likewise, she should have independent legal counsel before signing such a waiver.

It may be that a religious on exclaustration from her institute is seeking this consecration from the diocesan bishop. Since she is still legally bound to her religious institute by the bond of religious profession, she must petition CICLSAL for a transfer to this form of consecrated life. In this case the bishop or his vicar for religious should consult with the major superior of the religious institute regarding the life and behavior of the religious in the institute.

At times widows seek this consecration. Since there is no provision for the consecration of widows in the *Code of Canon Law* as in the Code of Canons of the Eastern Churches (CCEO, c. 570), a widow could be encouraged to discuss this way of life with her spiritual director or pastor. A suitable widow could certainly make a private vow of chastity and offer a service in accord with her gifts to her parish or diocese. It should be carefully explained to her that the Order of Virgins is for those who have never married. Also, a diocesan bishop interested in a rite of consecration for widows should petition the Congregation for Divine Worship to consider the institution of such a rite.

HELPFUL REFERENCES

- German Bishops' Pastoral, "Consecrated Virgins in the World." Translated by R. Barringer, *Canadian Catholic Review* (January 1988) 17-19.

- Holland, Sharon. "Consecrated Virgins for Today's Church." *Informationes* 24/2 (1998) 72-91.

- McDonough, Elizabeth. "Hermits and Virgins." *Review for Religious* (1992) 303-308.

- SCDW, *Sacrosanctum Concilium 80,* May 31, 1970; *AAS* 62 (1970) 650; *CLD* 7:421-425.

- Selvaggi, T. "An Ancient Rite Restored-Consecrated Virgins Living in the World." *Canadian Catholic Review* (January 1987) 6-11.
- www.consecratedvirgins.org.

COMMITMENT AND CONSECRATION
INTO THE ORDER OF VIRGINS

I, _____, commit myself with firm resolution to strive for my entire life to fulfill the lifestyle of one consecrated in the Order of Virgins according to the liturgical rite and canonical requirements of the Roman Catholic Church. As a consecrated virgin, I promise to deepen my prayer, my love for God and others, and to become more of a servant in the Church.

Under the guidance of my spiritual director, I will strive to live according to the Secular Franciscan Order of which I am a professed member. In this lifestyle I have promised to follow the Gospel way of life as articulated in the Constitutions. These norms call me to a life of prayer, penance, and service in the Church.

I understand that my vocation to a consecrated life of virginity is subject to the canons and discipline of the Roman Catholic Church in the interest of my personal salvation and spiritual development without hope or expectation of compensation in this life. Neither the Church nor the Archdiocese of _____, its clergy or other persons whatsoever have any financial responsibility to me nor to anyone else in compensation for my lifestyle or for the activities I may perform in striving to complete this spiritual journey.

_____
Signature

_____
Date

_____
Archdiocese

Case 12

The Approval of New Forms of Consecrated Life
Canons 576 and 605

Case

A priest asks for an appointment with the archbishop of a large metropolitan diocese. He is eager to gain approval for a new form of consecrated life which he believes is an inspiration of the Holy Spirit. The form will embrace clerics, religious, and the laity, both married and single. Its purpose is to go forth and evangelize people in city streets, parishes, educational, health care, and social service institutions. Fourteen or fifteen persons are interested in this new form and are scattered in many dioceses in the United States and South America. The priest asks the diocesan bishop for his support and eventual approval. What are some points the diocesan bishop should keep in mind and share with the priest during the interview?

QUESTIONS PERTINENT TO THE CASE

1. Is the priest a member of the Church in good standing? In what diocese or institute is he incardinated? Does he have permission from his ordinary to pursue this proposal?
2. What is the breakdown and canonical status of the fifteen persons associated with the project? How are they supporting themselves, and what are their living conditions?
3. At what times do they meet in order to sustain the *communio* among them?
4. How do they go about "evangelizing" in these various places described by the priest; does he insist on any formal education of these persons?
5. How have they been received in these places; has the priest any testimonials to their performance?
6. Has the priest a description of the nature, spirit, and goals of this inspiration, and what does he see that is new or original about it?
7. Has he attempted to write statutes or any norms for his associates?
8. Does he desire the institute to be a new form of consecrated life; if so, does he recognize that the Apostolic See must approve it?

9. Why has he come to this particular bishop, since the members are in various dioceses in the U.S. and South America?
10. Does the bishop recognize the description of the priest's inspiration as one of the traditional forms of consecrated life as described in the *Code of Canon Law* (religious institute, a secular institute, society of apostolic life)?
11. What support does the priest anticipate from the bishop at this time?

THE LAW

> Can. 576 It is for the competent authority of the Church to interpret the evangelical counsels, to direct their practice by laws, and by canonical approbation to establish the stable forms of living deriving from them, and also, for its part, to take care that the institutes grow and flourish according to the spirit of the founders and sound traditions.

> Can. 605 The approval of new forms of consecrated life is reserved only to the Apostolic See. Diocesan bishops, however, are to strive to discern new gifts of consecrated life granted to the Church by the Holy Spirit and are to assist promoters so that these can express their proposals as well as possible and protect them by appropriate statutes; the general norms contained in this section are especially to be utilized.

COMMENTARY

At present there are five forms of consecrated life approved by the Church: religious institutes (c. 607), secular institutes (cc. 710-712), societies of apostolic life (c. 731), the eremitical life (c. 603), and the order of virgins (c. 604). The Church understands her role in approving new forms of consecrated life (cc. 576, 605); and she respects and promotes the variety of institutes inspired by the Holy Spirit over the centuries (c. 577). The latest form of consecrated life to be approved by ecclesiastical authorities is the secular institute approved by Pope Pius XII in 1947.

In interviewing the priest, the bishop should ask the questions above and listen attentively to the type of institute or association father describes. Does he see some of the members living common life and professing the three evangelical counsels of chastity, poverty, and obedience as in religious institutes (c. 607 §2)? Will some other men and women live their separate lives in the world, evangelizing it in various ways and remaining in communion with one another through the living out of the spirit of this new form? Or does he envision some of these men and women will assume the evangelical counsels through sacred bonds described in canon law as those for secular institutes (cc. 710-712)? Or does he see the members living a life of charity in common and in accord with the counsels with hearts and minds directed to the apostolic commitments of the foundation as in societies of apostolic life (c. 731)? Since the priest envisions a group of persons, both men and women, with an apostolic purpose, there is no need to consider the eremitical life (c. 603) nor the order of virgins (c. 604) to the priest.

If after the bishop explains the canonical requirements for institutes and societies already existing in the Church, the priest insists he is being inspired to bring a new form into existence, he should describe his proposal for the bishop in detail. As the bishop listens, he would have the general norms on consecrated life in the Code of Canon Law to guide him (cc. 573-606). For example, one of the essential characteristics of consecrated life is the living a life of charity through the evangelical counsels (cc. 599-601, VC 12). While there are variations of poverty and obedience depending on the nature of the institute, there are no such degrees of the vow of consecrated chastity which obliges to perfect continence in celibacy (c. 599). Therefore, it would seem if the priest desires some form of consecrated life, be it one already approved or a new form, the married persons and single laity not willing or unable to commit to a celibate life in perfect continence would be associated with rather than members of the proposed institute of consecrated life.

Another consideration would be the fact that the priest envisions men, clerics and lay, and women, religious and lay, part of the new form. Where will the priests be incardinated; in a diocese or in the institute? This would largely depend on the way the priest envisions his institute. Also, there has been a precedent in the history of the Church that men and women religious shared the same constitutions under the authority of the one supreme moderator. However, prudence dictated separate living quarters and local superiors of both men and women in the houses of these religious. The bishop should also be aware of the many postconciliar Catholic movements and communities of the Christian faithful favored by John Paul II.

As the bishop listens to the priest, it would seem that there are two concerns he should keep in mind. The first would be to study carefully if the priest seems to be duplicating a form that already exists in the Church. Ecclesiastical authorities have been careful through the centuries to avoid such duplications and to recommend that persons re-presenting such gifts join those already in existence. Second, it seems a bit unwise at the fledgling beginnings of this association to have the members spread so thin in two continents. The candidates deserve a solid foundation in the consecrated life and the vision of this founder; likewise, they need to experience the challenge and support of one another in common life, if such be an essential of the proposed new form of consecrated life. Often in an attempt to gain members, new communities scatter their membership throughout a nation or the world. It would be important from the start that even or especially those aspiring to live some form of consecrated life, such as a secular institute without common life, be formed in the spirit of the founder. Only in such a way will the spirit be integrated into the lives of the members and attract others. Otherwise, it would seem that such candidates could meet the fate of the seeds in the Gospel parable scattered along the path, and among rocks and thorns.

- DePaolis, Velasio. "The New Forms of Consecrated Life." *Consecrated Life* 19/2 (1996) 62-85.

- Galante, Joseph A. "Consecrated Life: New Forms and New Institutes." *CLSA Proceedings of the Forty-eighth Annual Convention (October 13-16, 1986).* Washington, D.C.: CLSA, 1987: 118-125.

- McDonough, Elizabeth. "New Communities." *Review for Religious* (1993) 140-146.

- *"Movements" in the Church.* Edited by Alberto Melloni. *Concilium* (2003/3). See especially the articles by Melloni, Pace, Ganoczy, Durand and Lehmann.

- Neri, Antonio. "Nuove forme di Vita Consacrata. I profili giuridici." *Commentarium pro Religiosis Missionariis* 75/3-4 (1994) 253-308.

Case 13

The Canonical Election of a Major Superior in a *Sui Iuris Monastery*
Canons 615; 625, §2; 628 §2, §3

Case

The first councilor of a monastery of women religious in the diocese calls the office of the bishop. She advises his secretary that in two months the canonical election of the prioress will take place. She requests that the nuns have Mass on the day of the election and reminds the secretary that the diocesan bishop presides at the election in their monastery. What would be some issues the diocesan bishop should be aware of personally or through his vicar for religious prior to the election of the major superior of the monastery?

QUESTIONS PERTINENT TO THE CASE

1. Is it clear that the monastery is *sui iuris* and not a *non sui iuris* monastery with a major superior besides the superior of the monastery?
2. Is there a male superior (regular) that has true authority over the *sui iuris* monastery and has the right to preside at the election of the major superior?
3. How many nuns are in the monastery? What are their ages, dates of profession? Do all have both active and passive voice?
4. Does the bishop or his vicar for religious have a copy of the proper law of the monastery?
5. Is the bishop familiar with the election process; how does it differ from the canonical election provided in canons 164-179?
6. Which term is this for the present major superior; is she eligible for another term of office?
7. Is postulation permitted in the proper law; is it prohibited by the proper law?
8. Are there any sisters in perpetual profession having only active voice; are there restrictions on any members regarding election to office (e.g., nuns in temporary profession, extern or lay nuns)?
9. When was the last time the diocesan bishop or his delegate visited the monastery?
10. Based on the visitation records in the chancery or office of vicar for religious,

65

are there any concerns the diocesan bishop would have as he prepares to preside at the election?

Can. 615 An autonomous monastery which does not have another major superior besides its own moderator and is not associated to another institute of religious in such a way that the superior of the latter possesses true power over such a monastery as determined by the constitutions is entrusted to the special vigilance of the diocesan bishop according to the norm of law.

Can. 625 §1. The supreme moderator of an institute is to be designated by canonical election according to the norm of the constitutions.
§2. The bishop of the principal seat presides at the elections of a superior of the autonomous monastery mentioned in can. 615 and of the supreme moderator of an institute of diocesan right.

Can. 628 §2. It is the right and duty of a diocesan bishop to visit even with respect to religious discipline:
1° the autonomous monasteries mentioned in can. 615;
2° individual houses of an institute of diocesan right located in his own territory.
§3. Members are to act with trust toward a visitator, to whose legitimate questioning they are bound to respond according to the truth in charity. Moreover, it is not permitted for anyone in any way to divert members from this obligation or otherwise to impede the scope of the visitation.

COMMENTARY

Presiding at the canonical election of the major superior of the *sui iuris* monastery is one of the ways in which the diocesan bishop exercises his vigilance over monasteries described in canon 615 above. First, however, it would be important for him to know the canonical status of each of the monasteries in his diocese and his relationship to them. Is this truly a *sui iuris*, monastery, i.e., a monastery that does not have another major superior besides its own moderator and is not associated to another institute of religious so that the superior of the latter possesses true power over the monastery (c. 615). For example, the Contemplative Nuns of the Good Shepherd live in monasteries subject to the supreme moderator of the Sisters of the Good Shepherd. Second, the diocesan bishop must be certain that, if the monastery is *sui iuris,* it is not associated to an institute of male religious whose major superior has authority over some of the *sui iuris* monasteries of nuns and presides at the canonical election (c. 614). For example, the master general of the Order of Preachers or his delegate presides over the canonical election in some *sui iuris* monasteries of contemplative nuns of the Second Order.

Once the diocesan bishop or his canonist has determined the canonical status of the monastery, it would be wise to conduct a preliminary canonical visitation to become familiar with the nuns, to review with them the procedure for the canonical election, to answer their questions, and to foresee and address beforehand any problem that may impede a smooth electoral process.

It is important to petition the present major superior of the monastery for a list of the religious, their ages, dates of profession (first and final), their capacity or incapacity for active and passive voice, the term of the present major superior, and her eligibility for reelection. If there is no copy of the operative proper law in the chancery or office of vicar for religious, it would be well to ask for one before the visitation. The proper law would also inform if postulation (cc. 180-183) is permitted or prohibited. If there is no prohibition nor mention of postulation in the proper law, it would be permitted

The canonical visitation should take place well in advance of the day of election. Ordinarily, the nuns will inform the diocesan bishop of the pending election a month or so in advance. This affords time to set a date for both the canonical visitation of the monastery and the election. If it is not possible for the diocesan bishop to visit the monastery due to time constraints, it is important that he delegate his vicar for religious, a canonist, or another competent person familiar with the content of a canonical visitation (c. 628 §2, 1°, 2°, §3). The bishop or his delegate must respect and safeguard the monastery's right to autonomy of life accorded by the universal law (c. 586). However, the diocesan bishop's right to vigilance warrants questioning as to the regularity of the religious life of the monastery in accord with the proper law, the horarium, financial stability, and adequate provisions of spiritual, physical, and emotional care for the religious. He can inquire, too, as to the nuns' hopes for good leadership in the monastery to foster their life and witness of the contemplative life in the particular church.

Each of the nuns, the novices, and postulants should be interviewed, since they all contribute to the life of the monastery. At the end of the individual interviews, it would be well for the bishop or his delegate to meet with the nuns in the community room, advising them to bring their constitutions so as to review with him the procedures for election. If the nuns do not have questions, it would be well for the bishop or his delegate to review the norms on active and passive voice; postulation, if permitted; and the election process in general. It would also be important to determine what the proper law provides for an election: an absolute majority of those present (c. 119, 1°) or an absolute majority of valid votes cast ('17CIC, c. 101 §1), since some proper laws retain the latter. This information would be important, especially if there is a tie or a close election.

While the visitation may seem a bit tedious to the bishop or his delegate, it gives a message to the nuns of their importance to the diocese and prepares a smooth path for election day. It would be well for the canonist or one delegated for this visitation to accompany the diocesan bishop on the day of election, since he or she can answer any questions which may arise, particularly if he or she was delegated to do the canonical visitation..

It should be remembered that if a postulation is permitted by the proper law of the monastery, or at least, not forbidden, the nuns may postulate one of their own who would have a canonical impediment that is ordinarily dispensed (c. 180 §1). This happens particularly when the present major superior has completed the term or terms of office permitted in the proper law and is not eligible for an another consecutive term. At least two-thirds of the votes are required for postulation with the words *I postulate* (c. 181 §1). CICLSAL requires that postulation take place on the first or second ballot. It is important that the diocesan bishop or his delegate understand that if postulation occurs, and there is a two-thirds vote or more, the electoral process must stop.

The diocesan bishop advises CICLSAL of the postulation within eight days of the election (c. 182 §1). The cover letter should petition for a dispensation from the canonical impediment (c. 182 §1). Today, this can be done through the use of a fax machine. The congregation may reply by fax so the election can continue, but the rescript is ordinarily sent by mail. Once the dispensation is granted (even if the rescript has not yet arrived), the diocesan bishop informs the nun postulated who advises the bishop of her willingness to accept the postulation (c. 177 §1). If she accepts the postulation, she acquires the office immediately (c. 183 §3), and the nuns would then proceed to elect councilors for the monastery in accord with the norms of their proper law. The diocesan bishop is not obliged by law to preside at the election of the councilors.

HELPFUL REFERENCES

- McDonough, Elizabeth. "Authority in Institutes of Consecrated Life." *Review for Religious* 55/2 (March/April 1996) 204-208.

- "Nature and Purpose of General Chapters." *Consecrated Life* 2/2 (1976) 175-185.

- Smith, Rosemary. "Election of Major Superiors." *Bulletin on Issues of Religious Law* 8 (Spring 1992) 1-9.

LETTER OF DIOCESAN BISHOP TO ROME FOR POSTULATION

Date

Dear Cardinal _____ ,

On _____, I, Bishop _____ of the diocese of _____, presided at the canonical election of the major superior of the *sui iuris* monastery _____ in my diocese. Sister _____, the present major superior, who completed two terms of office in accord with the proper law of the monastery was postulated in accord with canon 180 §1 of the Code of Canon Law. Postulation is not prohibited by the proper law of the monastery. Sister received eleven of the twelve votes, exceeding the two-third vote require for postulation in canon 181 §1. She is impeded from accepting the election, inasmuch as the proper law of the monastery limits a major superior to two consecutive three year terms of office.

I recommend that the dispensation from this canonical impediment be granted for the spiritual and temporal well being of the religious community. Sister has given both witness and encouragement to the nuns in their contemplative lifestyle over the past six years in her office as major superior. Since the nuns are anxiously awaiting a response to their request for the dispensation from the impediment, I ask that a response be sent to my office by fax machine. I will notify sister of your decision and seek her acceptance of the office for another term of three years, so the nuns can continue with the election of the councilors. I understand that the official rescript will follow by mail.

Thank you, Cardinal _____ , for your kindness and consideration to me in my pastoral office on behalf of the religious and to the sisters in their request for the dispensation. With them I appreciate your concern for all those who have given themselves to the Lord through religious profession.

Fraternally yours,

_____

Bishop of _____

Case 14

Canonical Visitations of the Diocesan Bishop
to Churches, Apostolates, and Houses
of Religious Institutes
Canons 397, 628 §2, 1°, 2°, §3; 683

Case

*A recently installed bishop who has taken possession of his diocese is informed
that he has three religious institutes of pontifical right and eight religious institutes
of diocesan right represented in his diocese. He questions a canonist as to his
responsibilities in visiting the churches, apostolates, and houses of these institutes.*

QUESTIONS PERTAINING TO THE CASE

1. Are any of the pontifical right institutes *sui iuris* monasteries?
2. Does the bishop have a major site, i.e., the generalate or the provincialate of any
   of these religious institutes?
3. Will he personally make the visitation, or will he delegate his vicar for religious
   or another   ordinary to visit the houses, churches, and apostolates?
4. What would be some of the issues he would address or be aware as he visited
   the houses, churches, and apostoaltes of the religious?
5. Has he contacted any of the superiors of these institutes to date?
6. Has he announced or sent any explanation of his pending visitation?
7. Is there anything in the files in his office or the vicar for religious office
   regarding previous visitations?
8. Do the religious keep in regular contact with the office of the vicar for
   religious?
9. Is the bishop familiar with the charisms and spiritualities of the various
   institutes, with their proper works?
10. Do the religious have any works proper to them in the diocese; what are the
    works entrusted to them?

Can. 397 §1. Persons, Catholic institutions, and sacred things and places, which are located within the area of the diocese, are subject to ordinary episcopal visitation.

§2. A bishop can visit members of religious institutes of pontifical right and their houses only in the cases expressed in law.

Can. 628 §1. The superiors whom the proper law of the institute designates for this function are to visit the houses and members entrusted to them at stated times according to the norms of this same proper law.

§2. It is the right and duty of a diocesan bishop to visit even with respect to religious discipline:

1° the autonomous monasteries mentioned in can. 615;

2° individual houses of an institute of diocesan right located in his own territory.

§3. Members are to act with trust toward a visitator, to whose legitimate questioning they are bound to respond according to the truth in charity. Moreover, it is not permitted for anyone in any way to divert members from this obligation or otherwise to impede the scope of the visitation.

Can. 683 §1. At the time of pastoral visitation and also in the case of necessity, the diocesan bishop, either personally or through another, can visit churches and oratories which the Christian faithful habitually attend, schools, and other works of religion or charity, whether spiritual or temporal, entrusted to religious, but not schools which are open exclusively to the institute's own students.

§2. If by chance he has discovered abuses and the religious superior has been warned in vain, he himself can make provision on his own authority.

COMMENTARY

1. Visitation of *Sui Iuris* Monasteries and Religious Houses of Diocesan Right

The canonical visitation of major superiors and the diocesan bishop is an excellent way to show pastoral concern for the individual religious and to promote the spirit and life of the religious institutes in the particular church. The diocesan bishop has a special vigilance over *sui iuris* monasteries described in canon 615 and the houses of religious institutes of diocesan right present in the diocese. In both instances, he can visit the houses of these religious even with respect to religious discipline. On the other hand, he can visit the houses of religious institutes of pontifical right only as prescribed in the code (cc. 638, 683). Courtesy would prompt the bishop or his secretary to inform the religious prior to the visit.

Likewise, it would be well for the bishop to familiarize himself with the nature, spirit, and end of these institutes. For example, what are their distinctive spiritualities; are they of a contemplative or apostolic character? What special services do they render the particular church?

If the bishop has not been informed of any concerns regarding the particular monastery or house, the visit may be an ordinary pastoral visit. It would be wise to check with his vicar (priest) or delegate (male or female religious) for religious as the person delegated to visit the monasteries in order to gain this knowledge. If there are not serious issues, he could meet with all of the religious in the community room and advise them of his appreciation and dependence on their prayer or apostolic service, depending on their contemplative or apostolic character. At this time, he could ask if there is any particular need they have or any assistance that he or the diocese could offer them.

A study of canon 628 §2 reserves the visitation of *sui iuris* monasteries and houses of religious institutes of diocesan right to the diocesan bishop. In the latter case, this would be any house, i.e., generalate, provincialate, or local house of the institute located in his diocese. If the bishop decides that his vicar or delegate for religious would perform this task, he must delegate this authority or include it among the responsibilities of the vicar or delegate for religious at the time the priest (vicar) or male or female religious (delegate) is appointed.

If the visitation is to preside at the election of the general superior of an institute of diocesan right or the major superior of a *sui iuris* monastery, it would be well to precede the day of election by a canonical visitation so as to preclude any difficulties during the process of election. (See case on canonical election of a major superior in a *sui iuris* monastery). This visitation could be carried out by the bishop personally or by the vicar/delegate for religious Again, the bishop should be informed of any problem or concern.

If the visit is simply a pastoral visit to a religious house, it would be courteous to notify the religious superior of his intent and arrange a date and time for the visitation. This would ensure that the apostolic religious are present in the house of the institute of diocesan right and the nuns in the monastery can be alerted and prepared for the episcopal visit. Perhaps in the communication he would instruct as to what he sees as the reason for the visitation and the format it will take; here, too, he could inquire as to any particular concern that the religious may like to address. In this way, he avoids being caught off guard and can prepare to deal with the issue.

If there are concerns or an election is pending in a *sui iuris* monastery, he may wish to interview each religious followed by a general meeting in the community room. Individual interviews need not be in rank; the religious could sign up to meet with the bishop or his delegate. Questions could include: the quality of life in keeping with the spirit and purpose of the monastery, the freedom of conscience in approaching confessors, fidelity to the horarium, the good order of the house, the rules of cloister, the spiritual, emotional, and physical care of the members, the alms, labor, and temporal goods that sustain their life. Likewise, he may ask what qualities the individual religious recognizes as needed for leadership in the monastery. At the general meeting the bishop could exhort the religious to continue to grow in Christ and express his gratitude for the monastery recognized as a powerhouse of prayer in the diocese. Admittedly this is time consuming; in large archdioceses such visitations and be delegated to the vicar for religious.

The diocesan bishop likewise visits the houses of religious institutes of diocesan right. It would seem that, given the apostolic nature of these institutes and the fact that a major superior (general or provincial) visit them periodically, the visitation of local houses could be conducted in case of necessity or if there is a particular concern. If the general or provincial house is located in the diocese, the bishop or his vicar/delegate for religious may want to visit that major house once a year to be in contact with the major superior and the life and apostolic work of the religious institute. If there is a generalate of a diocesan right religious institute in the diocese, he would have further responsibilities towards that institute in addition to the canonical visitation (See cc. 595, 625 §2, 637 §1, §2). The election of the general superior would take place during the chapter of election, and he should be notified in good time to be present and preside over it.

During the bishop or his delegate's visit to either the monastery or house of diocesan right, the superior should be questioned as to whether there are any financial or other issues causing concern in the monastery or religious house. The bishop or delegate should have the annual account or report of the financial state of the house or monastery (c. 637) which should be reviewed before the visitation. There may be other concerns that the major superior would raise and the diocesan bishop could assist with diocesan resources. For example, there may be a *sui iuris* monastery which, due to aging members, can no longer provide hosts, vestments, or art work and be in financial straits. If these nuns have little or no patrimony or reserved funds, it may be difficult for them to sustain themselves with food, heat, prescriptions, etc. The diocesan bishop or his delegate may be able to procure help through the Catholic Charities, Knights of Columbus, or some other charitable avenue of funding in the diocese. He may also want the diocesan financial office to assist these religious in the administration of their temporal goods without undue interference in their autonomy of life (c. 586).

Visitation is particularly important for *sui iuris* monasteries, even more so than institutes of diocesan right. This is because they have but one moderator or major superior, whereas the diocesan institutes have, in addition to the supreme moderator, superiors or visitators delegated by the general superior who visit the individual houses. Likewise, the diocesan right institutes are apostolic; they have the financial security of regular stipends from the service of their members. The members are more apt to question or challenge unwise decisions of those charged with administration. Nuns living a contemplative life in the Church do not have the steady income of stipends; they depend on the revenue from their dowries, the work of their hands, and the alms given by thoughtful members of the Christian faithful. These religious in *sui iuris* monasteries are far more vulnerable, and the ordinary pastoral visitation of the bishop or his delegate should occur once a year, biannually, or at the very least before the election of the major superior takes place. If this is done faithfully, it will preclude serious problems for the monastery and grave heartaches and embarrassment for the diocesan bishop.

If serious concerns arise regarding a *sui iuris* monastery of pontifical right and the superior, having been notified, fails to take appropriate action, the diocesan bishop should render an account of his visitation, the problem(s), and his recommendations to the CICLSAL. If the nuns do not follow the bishop's recommendations, it would seem that the Apostolic See should intervene with its own canonical visitation of the monastery. Such a monastery could even be subject to the tragedy of suppression if the grave causes are not addressed, since the nature, spirit, and end of the monastery and its witness to the Christian faithful of the diocese are jeopardized.

While the diocesan bishop does not by law visit the houses of institutes of pontifical right that are not *sui iuris* monasteries; nevertheless, both he and these religious, particularly the major superiors, should endeavor to have good mutual relations. Therefore, it seems courteous and wise for the superiors to welcome him to the houses of the institute, particularly the generalate and provincilate of the religious institute, and he should indicate his willingness to visit the same. If there retirement or nursing facility for ill and elderly religious in the diocese, irrespective of the pontifical or diocesan right status of the institute, it would be gracious and kind for the bishop or his vicar to visit the facility occasionally, to offer Eucharist, and to extend the gratitude of the diocese for the many years of service accorded the diocese by these religious.

2. Visitation of Churches, Oratories and Apostolic Works

The bishop visits the churches and oratories frequented by the faithful as well as places of apostolic works (education, health care, social services) of all religious institutes, including those of pontifical right. A closer look at canon 683 indicates that this visit of churches, oratories, and apostolic works is an obligation resultant from the bishop's pastoral care of the people of the diocese entrusted to his care. The law obliges the bishop to perform the visitation annually in whole or in part, at least completing a visitation of the entire diocese within five years (c. 396). Included in this visit are persons, Catholic institutions, and sacred things and places located within the diocese (c. 397 §1). The bishop is to take care not to burden or impose hardship on anyone through unnecessary expenses during the course of the visitation (c. 398). Here again it would be wise for the bishop to communicate to the pastor, principal, or administrator of the institution his intent to visit. In this way, these responsible persons can prepare for the bishop and have time to raise any concerns or recommendations they may have for him.

Churches and oratories which the faithful regularly attend are included, since clerical institutes having his consent to erect a house in the diocese may also have permission to have a church in the diocese in a site determined by the bishop (cc. 611, 3°; 1215). Clerical religious may also administer a parish of the diocese. All religious have a right to an oratory in their houses (c. 608); if the lay faithful regularly attend services there, the oratory is subject to the ordinary's visitation.

In visiting churches and oratories frequented by the Christian faithful, the diocesan bishop should be interested if liturgical worship is carried on in keeping with the prescribed liturgical books. Likewise, he should observe the cleanliness of the places, the times for worship, the spiritual needs of people are addressed, and inquire from administrators as to any concerns or issues they may have. In the parish churches administered by members of institutes or societies, the diocesan bishop would review the baptismal register (c. 535 §2) and the books in which the records Masses, offerings, and intentions are recorded (c. 958 §2).

In addition to churches and oratories of these institutes, the diocesan bishop visits schools, health care institutions (nursing homes, assisted living houses, and hospitals) as well as social service institutions. When visiting schools, hospitals, nursing homes, and social service institutions, the bishop would be informed of any concerns by the principal of the school or administrator of the health care facility or social service institution. If any concerns have come to the attention of the bishop, he should raise them with the administrator or ask that they be rectified.

An account of all visitations should be kept in the files of the diocesan office. If the bishop or his delegate meets serious problems, he should call the attention of the competent major superior, pastor, principal, or administrator to the same. He can make recommendations and see that these are carried out.

HELPFUL REFERENCES

- Holland, Sharon. "Visitation in Religious Institutes: A Service of Communion." *CLSA Proceedings* 61 (October 1999) 161-178.

- McDermott, Rose. "Canonical Issues of Vicars for Religious: Ecclesial Dimensions, Community Life, Internal Governance." *CLSA Proceedings* 50 (1988) 139-158.

Case 15

The Responsibility of the Diocesan Bishop for the Finances
of a Religious Institute of Diocesan Right and a *Sui Iuris* Monastery
Canons 637; 638 §3, §4

Case

A recently ordained bishop has taken canonical possession of his diocese. He asks a canonist about his responsibility for institutes of consecrated life in his diocese. He is particularly concerned about the financial accountability of the diocesan institutes and sui iuris monasteries.

QUESTIONS PERTINENT TO THE CASE

1. How many members of institutes of consecrated life does the bishop have in the diocese
2. Are there any institutes of pontifical right in the diocese?
3. How many generalates, provincialates, and *sui iuris* monasteries are there in the diocese?
4. Does the bishop or his vicar for religious have copies of the proper laws of each of the institutes?
5. Has the bishop familiarized himself with the charism and patrimony of the institutes: their nature, purpose, spirit, and character, as well as their traditions (c. 578)?
6. Has there been a precedent of the bishop or his delegate meeting with the major superiors of these institutes at least once or twice a year?
7. Is there a council for religious that provides a forum for the religious to address the bishop regarding their concerns?
8. Are religious represented in the diocesan curia and in the various apostolates of the diocese?
9. Has the vicar for religious given the new bishop any account of the religious and the statistics of the respective institutes in the diocese?
10. Have the diocesan institutes and *sui iuris* monasteries been aware of their obligation of giving financial accounts to the diocesan bishop?

Can. 637 The autonomous monasteries mentioned in can. 615 must render an account of their administration to the local ordinary once a year. Moreover, the local ordinary has the right to be informed about the financial reports of a religious house of diocesan right.

Can. 638 §3. For the validity of alienation and of any other affair in which the patrimonial condition of a juridic person can worsen, the written permission of the competent superior with the consent of the council is required. Nevertheless, if it concerns an affair which exceeds the amount defined by the Holy See for each region, or things given to the Church by vow, or things precious for artistic or historical reasons, the permission of the Holy See itself is also required.

§4. For the autonomous monasteries mentioned in can. 615 and for institutes of diocesan right, it is also necessary to have the written consent of the local ordinary.

COMMENTARY

First it would be important for this newly installed bishop to understand and appreciate the basic autonomy of life enjoyed by all institutes of consecrated life once they have been approved by ecclesiastical authority as public juridic persons (c. 586 §1). As bishop of the diocese he is obliged to preserve and safeguard that autonomy (c. 586 §2). Second, he should distinguish between the institutes that are of pontifical right (c. 589) and those of diocesan right (cc. 589, 594). This distinction is important, since the institutes of pontifical right are subject to CICLSAL regarding internal governance and discipline (c. 594), while the institutes of diocesan right are under the special care of the diocesan bishop (c. 595).

Several norms in the Code of Canon Law point to instances in which the bishop's pastoral care is exercised over diocesan institutes and *sui iuris* monasteries in the diocese. These monasteries are those having no other major superior with authority over the monastery other than their own moderator (c. 615). The diocesan bishop in whose diocese these monasteries are located and/or in which the principal site or generalate of a diocesan institute is situated has more responsibility than a diocesan bishop who may have no *sui iuris* monastery and only local houses of religious institutes of diocesan right located in his diocese.

The following are two important provisions in the code that reflect a diocesan bishop's responsibility for the more important financial affairs of diocesan institutes and *sui iuris* monasteries in his diocese:

1. Financial Reports

Canon 637 addresses the annual rendering of accounts of the administration of *sui iuris* monasteries. Ordinarily, these monasteries have their own financial advisors or a competent member of the monastery who draws up the annual account for the diocesan bishop, the vicar for religious, or other designated ordinary in the diocese. Once received, the office of financial affairs of the diocese reviews this account and sends a memo containing his or her observations or recommendations to the diocesan bishop, vicar for religious, or the ordinary charged with this responsibility. If there are no problems, the bishop or ordinary sends a letter to the superior of the monastery expressing his appreciation for the report and the superior's financial responsibility. If there are concerns, these are stated in the communication to this major superior with a recommendation to take action. A copy of the report and letter of the bishop should be kept in the appropriate diocesan files so as to be certain that action was taken by the superior of the monastery.

The second part of the norm addresses the financial report of houses of diocesan right. These would be houses that are canonically erected as public juridic persons (c. 609), capable of acquiring, possessing, administering, and alienating temporal goods unless their capacity is excluded or restricted in the constitutions of the respective institute (c. 634). Most often these religious houses are generalates, provincialates, or large communities of local houses having a school or hospital attached. Other constituted local communities of religious residing in rectories or parish convents are not usually erected as public juridic persons. Often the religious communities in these latter houses tend to be small and manage temporal necessities with a budget submitted and approved by the general or provincial superior and monitored by the local superior and treasurer.

If there is a generalate, provincialate, or canonically erected house of religious of diocesan right in the diocese, the general, provincial, or local treasurer prepares the financial report for the information of the diocesan bishop or other appropriate ordinary (usually the vicar for religious). It would seem only if serious problems were raised by the diocesan financial officer would the bishop or other ordinary make recommendations to the competent superior of the institute, province, *sui iuris* monastery, or local house. The diocesan bishop would have the right to see that the serious problem had been addressed during the time of his canonical visitation of the religious house or monastery (c. 628 §2, 2°).

2. Alienation of Property

Canon 638 §3, §4 addresses valid alienation, i.e., the transfer or conveyance of the ownership of property belonging to the religious institute to another person or persons resulting in lessening or worsening the patrimonial condition of a religious institute. There must be a just cause to sell the property (c. 1293 §1, 1°), and the competent superior of the institute should obtain at least one, if not two independent appraisals (c. 1293 §1, 2°). While the appraisals are rather expensive and detailed, the petition should include the key elements of the appraisal(s). The provisions of civil law are to be observed (c. 1290). Besides the written permission of the competent superior with the consent of the council (c. 638 §3), the competent superior of a *sui iuris* monastery or diocesan right institute also requires the written consent of the local ordinary (c. 638 §4). Likewise, if the amount of alienation exceeds five million dollars and the annual adjustment amount as granted to the episcopal conference, the permission of the Holy See is required (c. 638 §3; Prot. n. AG 126-2/03). Finally, the praxis of CICLSAL requires the express opinion or *nihil obstat* of the diocesan bishop of the place wherein the property is located before the petition to alienate is granted.

In the alienation of property belonging to a diocesan religious institute, it is important to distinguish between two dioceses, i.e., the one in which the principal site of the institute is located, and the diocese in which the alienation takes place. It is the former (diocese of the principal site) in which the written consent of the local ordinary to alienate the property is sought. Only this local ordinary would be familiar with the financial condition of the entire institute. However, the *nihil obstat* of the bishop of the diocese in which the property to be alienated is located is also required. This latter requirement is not stated in universal law, but is the praxis of CICLSAL not only for institutes of diocesan right, but also for institutes of pontifical right. The bishop has a vigilance over the ecclesiastical goods in his diocese and may decide to purchase the property to keep it secure for church use. Or he may know some other church entity interested in purchasing it. Therefore, the major superior of the diocesan institute, the *sui iuris* monastery, and even the major superior of an institute of pontifical right must ask the diocesan bishop of the place where the property is located that is to be alienated if he has any objection to the alienation. This *nihil obstat* or "no objection" of the diocesan bishop should be in writing and included with the communications sent to Rome.

The letter of the supreme moderator of the diocesan institute petitioning to alienate the property should assure CICLSAL that all of the above requirements of canon law have been fulfilled (just cause, two appraisals, permission of competent superior with consent of the council, and all requirements of civil law {cc. 1290, 1293 §2}). He or she would enclose with the petition the two letters from the diocesan bishops. It would be well for the superior to petition that the property be sold for the lower appraisal indicated, since the amount petitioned will appear on the rescript when permission is granted. While the property must be sold for at least that amount, it can be sold for more than this stated amount. Sometimes, too, the superior can petition for the alienation of property "in principle." When the amount of sale is determined and CICLSAL is informed, this amount will appear on the rescript. When the rescript is received, the major superior will be informed that there is a *taxa* or charge for executing the rescript, and instructed that the money received from the sale of the proper must be used only for the reasons prescribed in law for ecclesiastical goods: 1) divine worship, 2) care for the ministers, 3) apostolic service, or 4) charity (cc. 1294 §2; 1254 §2).

It is important that the general or provincial council of religious institutes initiate this process as soon as the members of the institute agree to sell the property. In cases involving alienation time is money, and the delay in fulfilling canonical requirements before sending the petition to CICLSAL can hold up the rescript giving permission to sell. It would be invalid in canon law to proceed civilly without the required permissions. If there is a delay in the rescript, the major superior should call or fax CICLSAL. Ordinarily, that dicastery will advise by phone or fax that the petition has been granted, but the rescripts are always mailed. If the major superior receives word that the petition has been granted, then the religious institute can move on with the sale of the property.

HELPFUL REFERENCES

- DePaolis, Velasio. "Temporal Goods of the Church in the New Code, With Particular Reference to Institutes of Consecrated Life." *The Jurist* 43 (1983) 2:343-360.

- Hill, Richard A. "Financial Patrimony. *Review for Religious* 44 (1985) 140-144.

- _____ . "Patrimony Revisited." *Review for Religious* 49 (1990) 137-141.

- Hite, Jordan P. "Property Issues for Religious." *CLSA Proceedings* (October 1986) 139-142.

- Maida, Adam J. and Nicholas P. Cafardi. *Church Property, Church Finances, and Church-Related Corporations - A Canon Law Handbook.* St. Louis: CHA, 1984.

- Morrisey, Francis G. "Ordinary and Extraordinary Administration" *The Jurist* 48 (1988) 709-726.

- _____ . "The Alienation of Temporal Goods in Contemporary Practice." *Studia canonica* 29/2 (1995) 293-316.

- _____. "The Conveyance of Ecclesiastical Goods." *CLSA Proceedings* (1976) 123-137.

Part II

The Authority of Major Superiors and Chapters
in Institutes of Consecrated Life
Canon 586

The Church teaches that there are a great variety of institutes of consecrated life which have different gifts according to the grace given them (c. 577). Persons called to follow Christ more closely in the living out of these gifts or charisms are to observe faithfully the sacred patrimony of the particular institute through fidelity to its nature, purpose, spirit and character - all of which have been approved by ecclesiastical authority (c. 578).

The Church acknowledges an autonomy of life for each institute through which it possesses its own governance and discipline (c. 586). While general norms preserve and foster these institutes, much is left to the proper law of the institute for the ordering of its life and discipline. Superiors and chapters possess power over the members described in both the universal law and the proper law of the institute. In clerical religious institutes and societies of apostolic life of pontifical right, they also possess ecclesiastical power of governance for both the external and internal forum (cc. 596, 732).

Throughout the universal law, the authority of major superiors and chapters is evident. For example, the competent authority of the institute in accord with the norm of the constitutions divides an institute into parts, erects new parts, joins those erected, or redefines their boundaries (c. 581). The competent authority of the institute erects a house with the previous written consent of the diocesan bishop (c. 609 §1), and the supreme moderator can suppress a house after having consulted the diocesan bishop (c. 616 §1). The constitutions of each institute provide how superiors are elected or appointed to office (c. 623). These superiors are obliged to visit their members and houses in accord with their proper law (c. 628 §1).

A general chapter representing the entire institute holds supreme authority when in session. It is a sign of the unity and charity of the institute. Primarily, the general chapter: 1) protects the patrimony of the institute, 2) promotes suitable renewal according to the patrimony; 3) elects the supreme moderator, 4) treats affairs of greater importance, and 5) issues norms which all are bound to obey (c. 631 §1).

The autonomy of institutes of consecrated life and the authority of major superiors and chapters can be easily recognized in both universal law and in the proper laws of the institutes in the following areas: administration of temporal goods (cc. 634-640). The admission of candidates and the formation of members (cc. 641-661), the obligations and rights of the members (cc. 662-672), the apostolate of each institute (cc. 673-683), and separations from institutes (cc. 684-704).

Because of this just autonomy of governance and discipline of life, no canonist or other person should attempt to assist majors superiors or individual members of these institutes of consecrated life unless he or she studies Book II, Part III of the Code of Canon Law and the proper law of the particular institute. Part two of the manual presents cases in which the competent authority of the institute (major superior or chapter) resolves the issue in accord with universal law and the proper law of the institute. The format basically follows part one of the manual: a) a case, b) questions for clarification, c) the law, d) commentary, e) available documents, and f) helpful bibliography.

Case 16

The Right to Voice in a Religious Congregation
Canons 115 §1, §2; 171 §1, 1°, 2°; 172 §1, 1°, 2°; 631 §1, §2

Case

The general council of a large congregation of women religious received complaints from the membership that the nurses in their large infirmary were assisting the aged and ill religious in voting for chapter delegates. The administration appointed a sister to visit the infirmary and study the matter. She called a canonist for advice before undertaking her task.

QUESTIONS PERTINENT TO THE CASE

1. Is the institute of pontifical or diocesan right?
2. Approximately how many patients are assisted with voting?
3. What is the range of physical and mental illness of those being assisted in the infirmary?
4. What does the proper law of the religious institute state regarding active and passive voice?
5. Do the religious in the infirmary think that they must elect chapter delegates?
6. Are those nurses assisting the patients lay persons or members of the religious congregation?
7. Has there been any instruction given to the patients in the infirmary regarding the procedure for voting and their right to vote for the delegates?
8. How many complaints did the administration receive, and what were the issues?

THE LAW

> Can. 115 §1. Juridic persons in the Church are either aggregates of persons (*universitates personarum*) or things (*universitates rerum*).
>
> §2. An aggregate of persons (*universitates personarum*), which can be constituted only with at least three persons, is collegial if the members determine its action through participation in rendering decisions, whether by equal right or not, according to the norm of law and the statutes; otherwise it is non-collegial.

Can. 171 §1. The following are unqualified to vote:
1° a person incapable of a human act;
2° a person who lacks active voice;

Can. 172 §1. To be valid, a vote must be:
1° free; therefore the vote of a person who has been coerced directly or indirectly by grave fear or malice to vote for a certain person or different persons separately is invalid;
2° secret, certain, absolute, determined.

Can. 631 §1. The general chapter, which holds supreme authority in the institute according to the norm of the constitutions, is to be composed in such a way that, representing the entire institute, it becomes a true sign of its unity in charity. It is for the general chapter principally to protect the patrimony of the institute mentioned in can. 578, promote suitable renewal according to that patrimony, elect the supreme moderator, treat affairs of greater importance, and issue norms which all are bound to obey.
§2. The constitutions are to define the composition and extent of the power of a chapter; proper law is to determine further the order to be observed in the celebration of the chapter, especially in what pertains to elections and to the manner of handling affairs.

COMMENTARY

It should be kept in mind that religious institutes are public collegial juridic persons in the Church (cc. 115 §2, 634). Members direct the course of the institute through participation in rendering decisions either by direct vote or through delegates representing them at general or provincial chapters. All of the members should take the right and obligation seriously in electing delegates and sending recommendations to the chapter for the good of the institute.

The situation in the infirmary should be addressed with extreme sensitivity. There could have been little or no instruction prior to the voting, and the nurses may have been responding in charity to the requests of the infirm to assist them with their task. The sister visitator should advise the general administration that in the future it would be well for a member of the council or sister delegated by the general superior to visit the infirmary and instruct the ill and senior members of the institute.

An investigation could determine who among the patients are *non sui compos,* or incapable of the human act of voting. In such cases a statement from the doctor in attendance and the nurse caring for the patients could be kept on file to indicate the impossibility of the member to exercise her right to vote. This would preclude ballots filled in by well-meaning nurses who thought they were assisting the infirm in carrying out a duty of which they were incapable. It would also show the respect of the administration for the rights and obligations of the membership and sensitivity to those members incapable of carrying out this obligations. Never should a member be declared incapable of exercising active voice, unless he or she is judged incapable of placing a human act by competent professionals.

An instruction to the members in the infirmary who are *sui compos* and able to exercise their active voice would also facilitate matters in the infirmary. They should be advised that they have a right to vote for the chapter delegates, but there is no obligation to exercise that right. If the infirm or aged believe they have lost contact with a great many of the active members and the present needs of the institute due to their prolonged stay in the infirmary, there is no obligation on their part to exercise their right to vote. In fact, it may be more responsible to refrain from voting, if an infirm member thinks she does not know those members with the suitable qualifications for the deliberations of the chapter.

The sisters should understand that they should vote only for those whom they truly know to have the requisite qualifications. If the balloting calls for the election of forty persons, there is no need to vote for the entire number. The sisters should vote only for those whom they know would be exemplary delegates. The superior or councilor giving the instruction should assist the infirm with the knowledge that they have a right to vote, but may choose to waive that right. Great emphasis should be place on the apostolate of prayer in the infirmary for the deliberations of the chapter.

It would be well also to have copies of the ballot distributed among the infirm before the actual voting, and for the visitator or delegate to review the procedures in the proper law and those on the ballot sheet for the infirm and senior members. The delegated sister should be patient in responding to questions, aware of the difficulties of aging. The infirm should be knowledgeable and comfortable with their personal decisions in the matter. It would be well for the nurses to attend the meeting so as to hear the input and know their own responsibility in this matter. It can be a teaching moment for all concerned on the nature of the institute, and the rights and obligations of the members in this particular matter. Above all, it is a wonderful opportunity to let the infirm know the appreciation and respect of the administration for them as esteemed and responsible members in their twilight years of prayer and service to the institute.

HELPFUL REFERENCES

- Azevedo, Marcello De Carvalho. "Discernment and Elections in Religious Institutes." *Review for Religious* 48/5 (September-October 1989) 711-726.

- Darcy, Catherine C. "Models of Participation in Religious Community Chapters." *CLSA Proceedings* (October 16-19, 1995) 181-200.

- Holland, Sharon. "Visitation in Religious Institutes: a Service of Communion." *CLSA Proceedings* (October 4-7, 1999) 161-178.

- Radcliffe, Timothy. "Towards a Spirituality of Government." *Religious Life Review* 36 (July-August 1997) 199-213.

Case 17

The Election of a Brother as Major Superior in a Clerical Religious Institute
Canons 588 §1, §2; 623

Case

Two months prior to the provincial chapter, the major superior of a clerical religious institute calls a canonist. He advises the canonist that the men in the province seem to insist on nominating and electing a brother as provincial superior during the chapter of elections. The constitutions state that only a priest can be validly elected provincial superior. Since the major superior is not a canonist, he is not certain how to address this issue in the province.

QUESTIONS PERTINENT TO THE CASE

1. Is the institute of diocesan or pontifical right?
2. Is the major superior the provincial superior or the superior general of the institute?
3. Have the constitutions been approved by CICLSAL or by the bishop in which the generalate is located?
4. How has the major superior arrived at the conclusion that the men seem insistent on nominating and electing a brother?
5. Do they have one or more alternative nominees who are priests if they should be prohibited from their first choice for provincial superior?
6. What offices can the brothers be elected or appointed to in the institute in accord with the proper law?
7. Why do the men prefer a brother and this particular brother?
8. How many religious are in the province; what is the breakdown of clerics and lay members?
9. If this major superior is the provincial superior, has he notified the general superior of this possibility during the electoral process?
10. What was the reaction of the general superior; did he offer any advice?

Can. 588 §1. By its very nature, the state of consecrated life is neither clerical nor lay.

§2. That institute is called clerical which, by reason of the purpose of design intended by the founder or by virtue of legitimate tradition, is under the direction of clerics, assumes the exercise of sacred orders, and is recognized as such by the authority of the Church.

Can. 623 In order for members to be appointed or elected validly to the function of superior, a suitable time is required after perpetual or definitive profession, to be determined by proper law, or if it concerns major superiors, by the constitutions.

COMMENTARY

This is a very sensitive issue, since many clerical religious institutes want a fundamental equality for the lay and clerical members of their institutes. However, the universal law of the Church describes a clerical religious institute as one under the direction of clerics (c. 588 §2). Likewise, the constitutions of these clerical institutes and the praxis of CICLSAL preclude brothers from being elected or appointed to the office of major superior because of the jurisdiction accorded superiors of clerical institutes of pontifical right (cc. 596 §2, 620). On the other hand, some constitutions and permit brothers to be local superiors and councilors at each level of the institute (houses, districts, regions, provinces, generalate). If the provision for a brother to be a local superior is not permitted in the constitutions, an indult must be obtained from CICLSAL on a case by case basis in accord with the reasons presented.

After the major superior has responded to the canonist's questions, it would be well for the canonist to study the proper law, particularly the constitutions in order to be familiar with the provisions in the law of the institute. This is a sensitive issue and the rights of the members to vote for whomever they judge most suitable should be honored. Unless the constitutions prohibit postulation, the canonist should explain that the chapter will be postulating the brother for the office of major superior in accord with canons 180-183. He or she should caution that CICLSAL does not readily dispense from this impediment as it does in petitions addressing age, years of perpetual profession, or completion of terms of office (c. 180 §1).

If the constitutions do not prohibit postulation, the capitulars or chapter body must postulate the brother on their ballots. He must receive at least two-thirds of the votes for the postulation to have force (c. 181 §1). The election must stop at this point, and the results of the first balloting must be sent to the general superior of the institute who would ordinarily confirm the election (c. 182 §1). Even if the institute is one whose supreme moderator can dispense from the constitutions, it would seem he would not be able to do so in this case because the law seems to be constitutive for clerical institutes (cc. 86, 588 §2, 596 §2). Therefore, he would have to send the postulation on to the CICLSAL.

If the dispensation is not given by CICLSAL, this fact is made known to the provincial chapter, and the capitulars have the right to elect another candidate (c. 183 §1). It is well for the chapter body to have one or more other nominees in addition to the brother who meet the clerical and other qualifications required for election to so important an office. The issue of jurisdiction remained unresolved by the conciliar fathers during the Second Vatican Council, but the issue is frequently addressed by clerical religious institutes with professed clerical and lay members sharing the same charism, rights, and obligation.

HELPFUL REFERENCES

- *PC* 15, *VC* 61.

- McDonough, Elizabeth. "Jurisdiction Exercised by Non-ordained Members in Religious Institutes." *Canon Law Society of America Proceedings* (1996) 292-307.

- Beal, John. "The Exercise of Jurisdiction by Lay Religious." *Bulletin on Issues of Religious Law* 13 (Winter 1997) 1-6.

- _____ "The Exercise of the Power of Governance by Law People: State of the Question." *The Jurist* 55/1 (1995) 1-92.

- Provost, James. "The Participation of the Laity in the Governance of the Church." *Studia Canonica* (1983) 417-449.

Case 18

Procedure for a Religious Institute of Diocesan Right
To Obtain Pontifical Right Status
Canon 589

Case

A religious institute of diocesan right requested information regarding the process for obtaining pontifical right status from the Congregation for Institutes of Consecrated Life and Societies of Apostolic Life. The canonist consulted addressed certain questions with the general superior of the institute and shared the information required for such a process by CICLSAL.

QUESTIONS PERTINENT TO THE CASE

1. Is the institute one of diocesan right; does the general superior have the decree from the diocesan bishop erecting it as such?
2. How long has the institute been in existence; how many novices, temporary and perpetual professed members are there?
3. What are the apostolic activities of the institute?
4. How many dioceses are served by the members; how many houses has the institute, and in what dioceses are these located?
5. Is the institute in debt; is it financially sound?
6. Has the proper law of the institute been revised in keeping with the provisions of conciliar and postconciliar legislation for religious institutes?
7. What is the opinion of the bishop of the diocese in which the generalate is located with regard to this decision?
8. Does the general superior have the support of the other bishops whose dioceses are served by the members of the institute?

THE LAW

Can. 589 An institute of consecrated life is said to be of pontifical right if the Apostolic See has erected it or approved it through a formal decree. It is said to be of diocesan right, however, if it has been erected by a diocesan bishop but has not obtained a decree of approval from the Apostolic See.

When the membership increases significantly and the apostolic services of a diocesan right institute spread over a number of dioceses, the institute may decide to petition CICLSAL for pontifical right status. An institute of diocesan right has the same relationship with the diocesan bishop of its principal seat as does the pontifical right institute with CICLSAL. However, the diocesan bishop of the principal seat of the institute must consult the other diocesan bishops of the dioceses where the institute has spread in approving constitutions and confirming changes introduced into them (c. 595 §1). Also, as long as the institute has diocesan right status, the diocesan bishop of its principal seat presides at the election of the supreme moderator of the institute (c. 625 §2), and the other diocesan bishops have certain responsibilities of vigilance toward the houses and members (cc. 628 §2, 1°- 2°, 637; 638 §4; 686 §3; 688 §2; 691 §2; 700). An institute of pontifical right is accountable for these internal matters to the Apostolic See (CICLSAL, c. 593).

When petitioning for pontifical right status, the supreme moderator should consult with the membership, since the change in status will affect the entire membership (c. 119, 3°). The supreme moderator and the council should indicate the reasons for recommending the change in juridical status. The recommendation for a change in status may have come from a member, a local house, a province, or the general council. Time should be allowed for the membership's understanding of the implications and discussion before presenting the proposal to the general chapter and then on to CICLSAL. Seeking pontifical right status is a free act of the institute. CICLSAL requires a history of the institute and the juridical steps leading to its erection as a diocesan right institute. In addition to information requested from the institute, the diocesan bishop of the principal seat and the other diocesan bishops where the institute has houses and members are requested to testify to the stability and discipline of the institute, the fidelity of the institute and its members to its patrimony, its liturgical and ecclesial dimensions, as well as its financial security.

HELPFUL REFERENCES

- Congregation for Institutes of Consecrated Life and Societies of Apostolic Life issued the following information.

Documents Required in View of Obtaining Pontifical Recognition
of a Religious Institute of Diocesan Right

1. A historical-juridical account of the religious Institute from its beginning (not

more than two or three pages). A copy of the document by which the ecclesiastical authority erected the religious Institute of diocesan right should be included.

The history of the Institute should include the following points: Name and surname of the Founder; purpose, date and place of the foundation; name of the Bishop who authorized its beginning in his diocese; names of the first members; erection, date and place of the first house of novitiate; name of the Bishop who erected it; number of the first novices and date of their admission to the novitiate; the same for the first members in temporary and perpetual private vows; who was the first Master of Novices; dates of the General Chapters celebrated; who approved the first text of Constitutions and when; apostolic activities of the Institute at the beginning and at present; development of the Institute in other dioceses; particular spirituality of the Institute; *in case of clerical Institute:* place where the members are studying for the Sacred Orders; other important happenings during the history of the Institute.

2. *Curriculum vitae* for the Founder and of the first Superior general of the Institute. Include clearly: name and surname; date and place of birth, of baptism and of confirmation; parents' name and surname; place where he made his elementary and secondary studies; date of entrance in the Association and of his temporary and perpetual private vows; date of election as first Superior General and the period for which he was elected; his situation at present or date of death. If the Founder is (or was) a member of a religious Institute, the following are to be also included: place where he made his ecclesiastical studies; date of his admission to the novitiate and to temporary and perpetual religious profession; date of his Sacred Ordination; what kind of permission he got to follow his foundation. *In case of a Foundress:* date of her admission to the novitiate and to the temporary and perpetual religious profession in her previous religious Institute and any dispensations granted to her.

3. Up-to-date statistics of membership: names and surnames of the perpetually and temporary professed members; number of novices and of postulants; age of the perpetually professed members; number of houses and names of the dioceses where the members are living and working.

   To have a diocesan religious Institute recognized as of pontifical right, the number of members required is about 80-100 professed of whom the majority are in perpetual vows.

4. Financial status: besides declaring any debts, if any, point only: a) the number of houses owned by the Institute; b) the sum of money (in USA dollars) in Banks.

5. A statement regarding the following points: a) any facts of an extraordinary

nature with reference to the Founder, such as visions, etc.; b) whether in the diocese where the Generalate is located, there exists already any other religious Institute with the same name and charism.

6. Description of the religious habit of a novice and of a professed member.

7. Eight copies of the Constitutions and the Directory, revised in accord with the Code of Canon Law.

8. Testimonial letter from the diocesan Bishop of the Generalate of the Institute and from the other Bishops of those dioceses in which the Institute is present. Such letters are to be sent directly to the Congregation for Institutes of Consecrated Life and Societies of Apostolic Life, together with the opinion of the same Bishops about the following items, namely: a) stability and discipline of the Institute; b) initial and on-going formation; c) ability to ensure a responsible government of a religious Institute of pontifical right, besides the present Superior General; d) administration of goods; e) liturgical and sacramental dimension; f) collaboration with the local Church.

If possible, please, forward to the Cash Office of the Congregation for Institutes of Consecrated Life and Societies of Apostolic Life a deposit equivalent to 500 US $ on account for the expenses of the entire process.

Case 19

General Chapter Report Sent to CICLSAL
Canons 592 §1, 704

Case

A brother has been elected to the office of supreme moderator in his religious institute. He understands from some of the capitulars in the general chapter that he is obliged to send a report on the institute to CICLSAL with the completion of the general chapter. However, he is uncertain if the report submitted to the general chapter by the general administration this past year is acceptable. He inquires of a canonist as to where he can find a description of the content of the report for Rome.

QUESTIONS PERTINENT TO THE CASE

1. Is the religious institute of pontifical or diocesan right?
2. What does the chapter report include?
3. Has the brother access to the circular letter of Cardinal Hamer, O.P. sent to all major superiors in 1988?
4. Is this letter on file in the office of the general secretary of the brother's institute?

THE LAW

Can. 592 §1. In order better to foster the communion of institutes with the Apostolic See, each supreme moderator is to send a brief report of the state and life of the institute to the Apostolic See, in a manner and at a time established by the latter.

Can. 704 In the report referred to in can. 592 §1, which is to be sent to the Apostolic See, mention is to be made of members who have been separated from the institute in any way.

Both paragraphs of canon 592 oblige moderators of institutes of consecrated life in their relations with the Apostolic See (CICLSAL). That dicastery or congregation welcomes the reports sent by the supreme moderators of institutes of consecrated life since the reports reflect the lived experience of consecrated life throughout the world. Likewise, they foster the communion of the institutes with the Apostolic See and alert CICLSAL to any difficulties a particular institute may be experiencing, for example, due to scarcity of members or financial problems. Paragraph two of the same canon obliges all moderators of these institutes to promote knowledge of the documents of the Holy See and to see to their observance. This obligation on the part of superiors promotes the spirituality and knowledge of the members through study and reflection on the teachings of the Church regarding the vocation to religious life.

Canon 592 obliges the respective superiors of both diocesan and pontifical right institutes. On January 2, 1988, Cardinal Hamer, O.P. sent a letter regarding the report required by canon 592 §1 to the supreme moderators of religious institutes and societies of apostolic life. The reports should be sent with the completion of the term of office of the general superior, or every six years if the same superior's term if for life. Ordinarily, the report is the one that the general council submits to the general chapter, an account of their stewardship during their completed term of office.

HELPFUL REFERENCES

• Circular Letter to the Supreme Moderators of Religious Institutes and Societies of Apostolic Life

Criteria for preparing reports which are to be sent periodically to the Holy See on the state of life in religious institutes and societies of apostolic life.

Prot. n. SpR 640/85

The Holy See has a special interest in the state of religious institutes and societies of apostolic life and is concerned about their spiritual and apostolic growth, for this reason it follows their different situations with special care.

Therefore, in order that its work of pastoral service may be carried out more effectively and adequately and that the communion of Institutes with the Holy See may be fostered in accordance with canon 592 n. 1, it is very important that this same Holy See should be informed as to the situation and life of religious institutes according to circumstances of time and place.

In this way the Holy See can be a participant in the Lord (cf. Rom. 12, 15) in the joyful and sorrowful events of the institutes, and whenever possible in different situations–offer pastoral assistance in an appropriate fashion.

Toward this end the Congregation for Religious and Secular Institutes wishes to propose certain criteria for the reports that the supreme moderators of Institutes must make to the Holy See.

1. The report which the supreme moderator must make periodically to this Congregation can be that which he/she has already presented to the general chapter of the institute, but in summary form.

If, however, the general chapter is not celebrated every six years, as is the practice in most Institutes, the report will still be sent at six yearly intervals according to the directions indicated below.

The supreme moderators of religious institutes and societies of apostolic life are asked to send the report for the first time after the celebration of the next ordinary general chapter of the institute or society.

2. This report should consist of the following:

a) a brief and summarized statistical report of the members, the houses, and those parts immediately dependent that form the institute;

b) in what manner the constitutions are received and valued by the members, how the authority of the Institute is respected, what is the relationship between superiors and members;

c) what pastoral activity and encouragement of vocations takes place; what hopes are there for future growth of the institute; what is the early and ongoing formation, with special reference to the principal criteria and essential elements of such formation;

d) how fraternal life in community is lived;

e) what the relationship is with the Holy See, with the local bishop (especially regarding the apostolate and the liturgy), with the Unions of Superiors General, with the National Conference of Major Superiors, mentioning in what ways the superiors at the different levels participate in the meetings and works of these Unions and Conferences;

f) the work of the Institute with regard to pastoral action, and the other works of the apostolate in conformity with the Institute's charism;

g) the economic condition of the institute, noting, at least in general fashion, if there are particular difficulties;

h) the more urgent difficulties that must be provided for with special care, especially those dealing with the life and apostolic works of the institute, and the departure of members (cf. can. 704);

i) any other facts or aspects that might be called for that would clearly show the real state of the institute, for the purpose of promoting fruitful dialogue with this Dicastery.

The Congregation for Religious and Secular Institutes, while awaiting these periodic reports, asks God's blessing on all religious institutes, societies of apostolic life, and on all their individual members.

Rome, 2 January 1988 in the Marian Year.

Case 20

The Advice and Consent of the Council
Canons 627, 127 §1

Case

A *recently elected general administration, the general superior and four councilors, requests the advice of a canonist regarding how they should proceed according to canon and proper law in making quality decisions for the institute. How should the canonist advise them?*

QUESTIONS PERTINENT TO THE CASE

1. Is the institute of pontifical or diocesan right?
2. Is it a clerical or lay religious institute?
3. How large is the institute; how many members, provinces and houses does it have?
4. What are the works of the institute?
5. Do all four councilors reside in the generalate with the major superior or do they live elsewhere?
6. Have the councilors specific roles or responsibilities in addition to the office of general councilor?
7. Is the general treasurer a member of the council?
8. Has the general superior given or mailed the canonist a copy of the proper law of the institute?

THE LAW

> Can. 627 §1. According to the norm of the constitutions, superiors are to have their own council, whose assistance they must use in carrying out their function.   §2. In addition to the cases prescribed in universal law, proper law is to determine the cases which require consent or counsel to act validly; such consent or counsel must be obtained according to the norm of can. 127.

> Can. 127 §1. When it is established by law that in order to place acts a superior needs the consent or counsel of some college or group of persons,

101

the college or group must be convoked according to the norm of can. 166, unless, when it concerns seeking counsel only, particular or proper law provides otherwise. For such acts to be valid, however, it is required that the consent of an absolute majority of those present is obtained or that the counsel of all is sought.

Can. 127 §3. All whose consent or counsel is required are obliged to offer their opinion sincerely and, if the gravity of the affair requires it, to observe secrecy diligently; moreover, the superior can insist upon this obligation.

COMMENTARY

The requirement that superiors have a council reflects and protects the collegial nature of a religious institute (c. 115 §2) and guards against unilateral decisions. The councilors in participating with the general or provincial superior in decision-making should act in accord with their consciences for the good of the institute and the mission of the Church. It is important, therefore, that they be wise, intelligent, experienced religious who are able to make independent judgments and give good advice to the superior to assist in quality choices for the institute or province. They are not "yes" persons, simply concurring with the opinions of the superior, but must study the issue and give advice or decide for or against an issue with integrity and intelligence. Likewise, the superior must understand that he or she has the responsibility of acting or refraining from so doing after having fulfilled the obligations of universal and proper law.

If the superior general and councilors do not know each other well, the canonist should advise that they meet informally over a meal or social and become more acquainted. Before or after a meal, they could share their concerns for the institute and how each recognizes his or her role as major superior or councilor. They should review the enactments of the recent general chapter and discuss how they could best implement them during their term of office. In other words, each would share his or her vision of how best to serve the members, the institute, and the Church in accord with the charism of the institute and the enactments of the chapter.

It would be important that the canonist review the universal law and the proper law of the institute, giving instances of when the advice or consent of the council is required. For example in the code, canons 638, §3; 647, §1, § 2; 656, 3°; 697, 699 §1 and 703 should be noted. Most probably these are included in the proper law, since ordinarily it would conform to the code. However, some proper legislation is stricter than the code in requiring consent rather than advice as prescribed in canon law. Likewise, some proper laws require consent or advice for other situations than those enumerated in universal law.

Unless the proper law provides otherwise, there is only one time in the universal law of the Church when a collegial vote of the general superior with the council is required for the validity of the act, i.e., for the dismissal of a member of the institute (c. 699 §1). In other instances either the advice or the consent of the councilors is sought. If the proper law provides a collegial vote at other times, e.g., the merging of two provinces or suppression of a canonically erected house, then the proper law must be followed. If a collegial vote is required, an absolute majority decided. In such a case, the vote has the force of law, and the superior is bound to act (c.119, 2°).

If the proper law requires the consent of the council, e.g., for the alienation of property (c. 638 §3), the competent superior must convoke the council and obtain the consent of an absolute majority of those present in order to act validly. In other words, if there are four councilors, the major superior must obtain the consent of three of the four for a valid act. If an absolute majority of the council agree to the alienation, this does not mean that the general superior has to act, but he or she is free to act validly.

If the advice of the council is required, the general superior must convoke the councilors and ask for their advice in order to act validly. The superior is not obligated to follow the advice of the councilors, but it would seem if they are unanimous in their opinion about some issue, the superior should be wary in going against this advice. In a few religious institutes, the proper law provides that the advice of the councilors can be obtained through a conference telephone call. With this provision, the general superior of large international religious institutes can visit the various provinces, houses, and members of the institute, while reserving major decisions requiring the consent of the council to formal convocations. Note that canon 127 §1 states "...unless particular or proper law provides otherwise..." when addressing the advice of the councilors. The provision for seeking the advice of the council in a conference call would have to be stated in the proper law of the institute.

Additionally, CICLSAL has permitted some institutes to provide in their proper law that councilors can give their consent by way of a telephone conference if the vote required is not secret (e.g., admission to vows, orders, offices). For a secret vote the councilors must be convoked, and a quorum of the council present. Unless the provision has been petitioned and approved in the proper law of the institute, a conference phone call cannot be employed when consent is required. The conference call permits each councilor to hear the opinions of the other councilors who share the best interests of the institute. It may happen that one councilor offers expert advice on the issue at hand, and his or her input would change the vote of one or more of the other councilors.

It is important to remember that having obtained the consent of three or perhaps all four councilors, the general superior is free to act validly, but he or she is not bound to act. It may be that she has been informed subsequently to the vote of the council that the property to be alienated would substantially increase in monetary value within six months or a year. In such a case, the competent superior may decide to wait out the six months for the financial increment for the institute. The point is that he or she is free to act, (not obligated to act) since the consent of the council has been given.

Regarding canon 127 §1, the Pontifical Commission for the Interpretation of Legal Texts was asked:

"Whether when the law requires that the superior must have the consent of the council or of a body of persons in order to act, in keeping with canon 127 §1, does the superior have the right of voting with the others, at least to break a tie?

On May 15, 1995, the commission responded in the negative. In other words, the superior does not have the right to vote with the others, even to break a tie. So if two councilors voted in the affirmative for an issue and two voted in the negative, the superior does not have an absolute majority of the councilors' votes and would act invalidly if he or she carried out the act.

One must also carefully distinguish between universal law with its authentic interpretation and what may be the approved custom of a religious institute. It may be that a religious institute, due to its tradition, has a more collegial interaction of the major superiors and the councils. If the constitutions have been approved by CICLSAL with these same provisions, then the proper law is followed. The congregation is very careful to honor the patrimony of religious institutes (c. 578).

Finally, it should be understood by the superior and councilors that they are professional persons in their roles of service to the members. Not only the grave affairs stated in canon 127 §3 should be held secret, but all matters discussed or deliberated on at council meetings should be kept confidential.

HELPFUL READINGS

- Andrés, D.J. "De superiore eiusque consilio." *Commentarium pro Religiosis Missionariis* (1987) 408.

- DePaolis, Velasio. "An Possit Superior Religiosus Suffragium Ferre cum suo Consiglio vel suo Voto Dirimere Paritatem sui Consilii." *Periodica* 76 (1987) 413-446.

- _____ . *La Vita consacrata nell chiesa.* Bologna: Centro Editoriale Dehoniano, 1991: 216-220..

- Hill, Richard A. "The Role of Councils and Councils Revisited." *Review for Religious* (1986) 140-144; 623-624; 933-935.

- McDonough, Elizabeth. "Religious Superiors and Government." *The Way Supplement* 50 (1984) 61-70.

- _____ . "Basic Governance Structures in Religious Institutes." *Review for Religious* (1990) 928-933,

- _____ . "Participation in Governance. *Review for Religious* (1991) 775-780.

- Neville, G.J. *The Religious Superior's Council in the 1983 CIC.* Doctoral Dissertation. Ottawa: St. Paul University, 1989: XVI + 248.

Case 21

All Members in Perpetual Profession
as Capitulars in the General Chapter
Canon 631

Case

The superior general of a clerical religious institute seeks the advice of a canonist. The major superior advises the canonist that there are currently fifty-five men in the religious institute. They would like to have universal suffrage, i.e., all of the perpetually professed members to have both active and passive voice at the next general chapter. However, the constitutions provide for five ex officio members and a defined percentage of elected delegates. How can the superior general respond to what seems to be the consensus of the members of the institute?

QUESTIONS PERTINENT TO THE CASE

1. Is the institute of pontifical or diocesan right?
2. How is the institute divided: provinces, regions, districts, houses?
3. Are the men and parts of the institute in close proximity to one another?
4. Has the institute ever been larger; was the decline in membership gradual or sudden?
5. How has the superior general become aware of the desire of the members for this change in the constitutions?
6. Would there be some members who would not be able to attend the general chapter?
7. How many members would be *non sui compos*, and incapable of voting?
8. Is the clerical institute composed of brothers as well as priests; does the law prohibit brothers from being capitulars or holding an office in the institute?
9. When is the next ordinary general chapter; what exactly do the constitutions state concerning the election of the delegates to it?
10. Has this recommendation of the membership been prompted by a downsizing of the institute and the close proximity of the members to one another; how is the canonist to understand a "consensus of the membership"?

Can. 621 §1. The general chapter, which holds supreme authority in the institute according to the norm of the constitutions, is to be composed in such a way that, representing the entire institute, it becomes a true sign of its unity in charity. It is for the general chapter principally: to protect the patrimony of the institute mentioned in can. 578, promote suitable renewal according to that patrimony, elect the supreme moderator, treat affairs of greater importance, and issue norms which all are bound to obey.

§2. The constitutions are to define the composition and extent of the power of a chapter; proper law is to determine further the order to be observed in the celebration of the chapter, especially in what pertains to elections and the manner of handling affairs.

§3. According to the norms determined in proper law, not only provinces and local communities, but also any member can freely send wishes and suggestions to a general chapter.

COMMENTARY

Canon 631 describes the general chapter, the supreme authority in the institute, its composition, and five principal responsibilities. The institute in question is rather small, composed of fifty-five men. It would first be important to know its canonical status, i.e. of pontifical or diocesan right. Since this dispensation from the constitutions of the institute would be one of eligibility for chapter membership, the diocesan bishop can grant the dispensation from the proper law for an institute of diocesan right (cc. 87 §1, 595 §2). If the institute is one of pontifical right, the petition for dispensation from proper law would be addressed to CICLSAL (593).

It lies within the competence of the general chapter to recommend changes in the constitutions by a two-third vote of the capitulars. Therefore, it would be important to know when the next general chapter takes place. If the chapter convokes within the next month or so, it would seem that a proposal to this effect should be carefully drafted and presented to the capitulars in order that it be voted on and the recommendation for a change in the constitutions be made to CICLSAL. The praxis of a two-third vote of the general chapter for such important measures as constitutional changes protects the members of the institute from precipitous or arbitrary changes in their fundamental code and their right of active voice in voting for delegates to represent them at the general chapter. A poll of the religious could precede the chapter so as to insure the support of the members for such an important change in the constitutions affecting them.

If the general chapter will not take place for six or more months, it would seem that the general administration could conduct a referendum of the membership to ascertain the percentage desiring this change in the constitutions. Since it is a point of law that "what touches all as individuals, however, must be approved by all" (c. 119, 3°), it would see that the greater majority of the membership would want this change in the constitutions. If the referendum supports the change, it would seem that the general superior could petition this reasonable request of the competent ecclesiastical authority on behalf of the membership so the change could be implemented for the upcoming general chapter.

Ordinarily, CICLSAL does not permit a change in the constitutions of the institute for this request, but grants an indult on an ad hoc basis to the religious institute whose membership is one hundred or less and the members in perpetual profession can be convoked for the chapter without too great expense or inconvenience. The institute is requested to send a brief report of the proceedings following the celebration of the general chapter to the congregation. It should be remembered that canon 119, 1° and 3° require that those decisions have the force of law which are approved by an absolute majority of the majority present of those who must be convoked.

The concerns of CICLSAL regarding requests for universal suffrage in the general chapter of a religious institute are: the possibility of lobbying or factions in large assemblies, the failure of capitulars to know one another and attain unity of hearts and minds, the inability of the capitulars to hear each one's views or opinions due to numbers, the disregard for the members' right to active voice in voting for suitable delegates to the chapter, and of having either only the quorum or not even that quorum present at the chapter required in canon 119, 1°.

HELPFUL REFERENCES

* *Canon Law Digest* 8: 354-357; 9:356-358, 364; 102-106.

* "Direct Suffrage for the Election of Major Superiors of Religious Institutes." *Consecrated Life* 3/1 (1977) 40-43.

* "Is it permissible to have direct election of supreme moderators and major superiors?" *Bulletin on Issues of Religious Law* 1/1 (November 1985) 5-7.

* Smith, Rosemary. "Election of Major Superiors." *Bulletin on Issues of Religious Law* 8 (Spring 1992) 1-9.

Case 22

Participation of the Membership in the General Chapter
Canon 631 §1, §3

Case

A member of the general council calls a canonist and advises that their general chapter will be held during the summer of the following year. The religious congregation numbers about twelve hundred religious, and the general superior wants the members to enjoy the broadest participation possible. How can this happen within the limits of universal and proper law?

QUESTIONS PERTINENT TO THE CASE

1. Is the institute of pontifical or diocesan right?
2. How many of the religious would be able to attend sessions of the general chapter without undue travel expense or inconvenience?
3. How long is the chapter in session; is the chapter of affairs separate and at a different time than the chapter of election?
4. What do the *Constitutions* of the institute provide for the composition and authority of the general chapter?
5. How many *ex officio* and delegated members are there in the chapter?
6. Is this an ordinary or extraordinary general chapter?
7. Does the institute have any provisions in its *Directory* or *Statutes* for observers, participant observers, or experts to the general chapter?
8. Is there a procedure in the proper law for the election of the delegates; do they truly represent the entire twelve hundred members?
9. Will the entire membership have opportunities to send proposals to the committee preparing for the chapter; is their a process for the membership to nominate religious for the general administration?
10. How long is the chapter in session; is there any provision for communication with the broader community during the chapter sessions through closed circuit tv, or e-mail or daily newsletters?
11. How are the enactments of the chapter published; is there any education of the broader membership regarding the rationale behind the enactments?

Can. 631 §1. The general chapter, which holds supreme authority in the institute according to the norm of the constitutions, is to be composed in such a way that, representing the entire institute, it becomes a true sign of its unity in charity. It is for the general chapter principally: to protect the patrimony of the institute mentioned in can. 578, promote suitable renewal according to that patrimony, elect the supreme moderator, treat affairs of greater importance, and issue norms which all are bound to obey.

§2. The constitutions are to define the composition and extent of the power of a chapter; proper law is to determine further the order to be observed in the celebration of the chapter, especially in what pertains to elections and the manner of handling affairs.

§3. According to the norms determined in proper law, not only provinces and local communities, but also any member can freely send wishes and suggestions to a general chapter.

COMMENTARY

The concept of a chapter body in which the members of a religious institute are convoked to discuss the patrimony of the institute and its renewal is rooted in monastic times. Benedictine monks met monthly in their monasteries to discuss a chapter of the Rule of Benedict and how they would live that particular aspect of their religious life more fully. Gradually, this convocation of the members for renewal and adaptation became known as 'chapters."

Orders and congregations of apostolic religious institutes have far different configurations than *sui iuris* monasteries. The chapter, whether composed of the professed members of the monastery or a representative body of professed members of a large centralized institute, shows the unity and love bonding the members. Recognizing this important concept, the general superior wants to assure the twelve hundred members as great a representation at the chapter as possible, understanding that praxis of CICLSAL does not permit direct universal suffrage or a so called "chapter of the whole" for institutes with more than one hundred members.

The general superior should announce the convocation of the chapter at least six months in advance of the event, invite members to send their proposals to the administration for the Chapter Planning Committee (c. 631 §3). A proposal should succinctly state the issue or the problem, address how it could be implemented or resolved, and firm up the implementation or resolution of the issue with some documentation for the chapter body to consider. The latter will add strength and credibility to the proposal.

The same communication should contain a list of those eligible to be elected as delegates to the chapter in accord with the constitutions. Ordinarily, these are members in perpetual profession. These religious could, after prayerful discernment, remove their names from the list if they are unable to commit to this service. The process for electing delegates should be carefully explained to the membership, i.e., the number to be elected or the percentage of votes needed for a member to be a chapter delegate.

Another consultative process whereby all of the membership can participate is the nomination of members having the qualities for the office of general superior. Twenty-five or thirty members receiving the highest number of nominations could be published for the general membership. This list would guide but not bind the capitulars, as they elect those they deem best suited for offices of service in the institute.

While CICLSAL insists on the chapter body as representative of the membership, i.e., with *ex officio* members and delegates according to the constitutions of the institute, there is no reason why observers and participant observers could not attend the sessions of the general chapter. Observers would have the advantage of listening to the discussions of the capitulars and carrying information back to their respective communities. Participant observers would take part in the discussions of the chapter body, but without a deliberative vote. Experts on various issues and non-delegates could be invited to assist the capitulars with such tasks as communication, logistics, typing, closed circuit tv, refreshments, etc., requiring additional help. If the capitulars believe there are sensitive matters that merit a closed session, they can always decide on the same which would include only the chapter body. It is important that they realize that, while in session, they are the supreme authority in the institute (c. 631 §1). Some institutes have a designated house of prayer where members volunteer to gather for prayer during the period of the chapter.

The general chapter of a religious institute is an ecclesial event, and it is recommended to institutes of pontifical right to invite the bishop or his delegate to celebrate the Eucharist on the day of the election. The bishop of the diocese presides at the election of the major superior in a *sui iuris* monastery of nuns and the election of the general superior in an institute of diocesan right. As many members as possible could participate in the Mass of the Holy Spirit. However, discretion should be employed with the attendance of all members or observers at the actual election, since often there is a process involving discernment and an announcement of the results of each ballot. It may be well to invite non-chapter members and other observers to pray outside the chapter room until an election takes place. Since the chapter will be held in the summer, perhaps a picnic lunch on the grounds of the generalate would be a fitting communal celebration concluding this important event in the life of the institute.

HELPFUL REFERENCES

* De Carvalho Azevedo, Marcello, S.J. "Discernment and Elections in Religious Institutes." *Review for Religious* 48/4 (Sept./Oct. 1989) 711-726.

* Darcy, Catherine C., R.S.M. "Models of Participation in Religious Community

Chapters." *CLSA Proceedings* (October 16-19, 1995) 181-200.

- "Direct Suffrage for the Election of Major Superiors of Religious Institutes." *Consecrated Life* 3/1 (1977) 49-43.

- Harmer, Catherine. "Chapters Present and Future." *Review for Religious* 53 (1994) 120-129.

- Hill, Richard A., S.J. "Autonomy of Life." *Review for Religious* (1986) 781-784.

- McDonough, Elizabeth, O.P. "General Chapters: Current Legislation." *Review for Religious* 54 (1996) 431-435.

- _____ . "General Chapters: Historic Background." *Review for Religious* 55/3 (1996) 320-325.

- "Nature and Purpose of General Chapters." *Consecrated Life* 2/2 (1976) 175-185.

- Radcliffe, Timothy, O.P. "Towards a Spirituality of Government." *Religious Life Review* 36 (July/August 1997) 199-213.

- Smith, Rosemary, S.C. "Election of Major Superiors." *Bulletin on Issues of Religious Law* 8 (Spring 1992) 1-9.

Case 23

The Treasurer of a Province of a Religious Institute
Canon 636

Case

A *clerical religious calls a canonist for advice. He has been appointed treasurer of a rather large province of his religious order. While he has a background in finances, he is not familiar with canonical norms for his new assignment in the province. How should the canonist prepare to meet with the priest and given the requested advice?*

QUESTIONS PERTINENT TO THE CASE

1. Is the religious institute of pontifical or diocesan right?
2. What does the religious mean by a "rather large province"?
3. Will he have a finance advisory council, and what are their ranges of experience?
4. Did the former treasurer offer him any assistance?
5. Did the former treasurer have membership in NATRI?
6. Are there any immediate concerns other than the canonical issues he has as treasurer?
7. Is the office of treasurer separate from the provincial council, or is he a member of the provincial council?
8. What apostolic work did the priest perform prior to being appointed provincial treasurer?
9. In his opinion, does the province manage the temporal goods in keeping with the poverty of the institute?
10. Does he recognize that all of the temporal goods of the institute are ecclesiastical goods and are governed by Book V of the Code of Canon Law?
11. Does the institute have recourse to civil law counsel?
12. Has he studied the proper law of the institute regarding its temporal goods and the role of the provincial treasurer?
13. Is the province of the institute incorporated as a not-for-profit corporation in civil law?

14. Has he studied the articles of incorporation to insure that the province follows the provisions in civil law?
15. How many other corporations does the province have; does he know the civil requirements for their fiscal accountability?

THE LAW

> Can. 636 §1. In each institute and likewise in each province which is governed by a major superior, there is to be a finance officer, distinct from the major superior and constituted according to the norm of proper law, who is to manage the administration of goods under the direction of the respective superior. Insofar as possible, a finance officer distinct from the local superior is to be designated even in local communities.
> §2. At the time and in the manner established by proper law, finance officers and other administrators are to render an account of their administration to the competent authority.

COMMENTARY

Since this financial officer is unfamiliar with canon law, it may be well at the meeting to focus on issues regarding temporal goods in the proper law of his institute and the Code of Canon Law, particularly canons 634-640 and Book V on the Temporal Goods of the Church. With this overview of the law on temporal goods, particularly those directed to the financial officer of a religious institute, he will have some initial understanding of the duties of his office. It is important that he recognize there are parameters around his office; he is always accountable to the superior of the province, and he carries out the ordinary administration of the temporal goods. Therefore, it would be important that he have a copy of the proper law of the institute and the statutes and/or policies of the particular province in order to determine what is understood by ordinary administration in the institute. He should review these documents to determine the times and the manner he must render an account of his administration to the provincial superior (cc. 636 §2, 638 §2). Many institutes also insist on an account being rendered to the membership of the institute or the province.

The proper law should also provide for the extraordinary administration of the province and what is necessary to place such an act (c. 638 §1). Acts of extraordinary administration often require the permission of the competent superior before they can be placed validly. Furthermore, alienation and any act which threatens the patrimonial condition of the province would require the written permission of the competent superior (general or provincial) and the consent of the council. If the amount exceeds that determined by the Apostolic See, or items given to the Church by vow, or those precious for historical reasons, the permission of CICLSAL is also required (c. 638 §3).

The code further requires a public juridic person such as a province of a religious institute to have a finance council (c. 1280) to assist the financial officer in carrying out his responsibilities. These persons are expert in finances, civil law, property, development, or insurance; they offer advice to the treasurer and provincial superior and council. They need not necessarily be members of the institute, and should never be confused with the provincial council that gives advice and consent to the superior in accord with universal and proper law on issues relating to the temporal goods of the institute.

Another significant canon for the finance officer is canon 1284 which describes the role of the administrator of a public juridic person. While the administrator of a diocese or a religious institute or province would be the one in charge, e.g., the diocesan bishop or major superior; nevertheless, the financial officer performs many of the tasks in this canon and renders an account to the provincial superior.

If the office of treasurer has been well managed prior to this priest's appointment, it would seem the institute enjoys membership in NATRI (http://ww.natri.org. and the Legal Services Office of the CMSM/LCWR. These offices in Silver Spring, MD prove most helpful, particularly to newly appointed or elected treasurers of religious institutes. At their workshops, the priest will meet up with seasoned treasurers whom he can call for advice. They publish excellent articles on significant issues connected to the office of treasurer and temporal goods in religious institutes. Today, there are many complex issues with health care, insurance, retirement plans, financial portfolios, and canon and civil law issues that need the attention of experts. Communicating with these offices puts the new treasurer in a position to become acquainted with and rely on experts for advice.

The treasurer should understand the nature of the vow of poverty the members of his institute have made (cc. 600, 668). If the institute does not require the renunciation of personal goods (c. 668 §4), and some members entrust the institute with the administration of their patrimonies, he should understand the proper law in this regard and keep these personal goods of the members separate from the temporal goods of the institute. Taxes are to be paid on such individual patrimonies, and an account must be rendered to the competent civil authorities in this regard.

Most of all, it is important that the treasurer recognize he holds an ecclesiastical office (c. 145 §1), inasmuch as the temporal goods of the Church are used for: divine worship, the care of the ministers, apostolic works, and charity (c. 1254 §2). As a trustworthy steward, he should be sensitive to the needs of the members of the province, the financial stability of the institute, and charity in addressing the needs of the Church and the poor. (c. 634 §2, 635 §2, 640).

HELPFUL REFERENCES

- DePaolis, Velasio. "Temporal Goods of the Church in the New Code with Particular Reference to Institutes of Consecrated Life." *The Jurist* 43 (1983) 343-360.

- Leonard, Joan De Lourdes, C.S.J. "Temporal Goods Canons 634-640." In

Religious Institutes, Secular Institutes, Societies of Apostolic Life: Handbook on Canons 573-746: 99-114. Edited by Jordan Hite, et al. Collegeville, MN: The Liturgical Press, 1985: 99-114.

• Morrisey, Francis G. "The Alienation of Temporal Goods in Contemporary Practice." *Studia Canonica* 29 (1985) 293-316.

• Smith, Rosemary. "Temporal Goods and their Administration [cc. 634-640]." In *New Commentary on the Code of Canon Law*: 797-805. Edited by John P. Beal et al. Washington, D.C.. Canon Law Society of America, 2000.

Case 24

Alienation of Property of a Religious Institute
Canons 638 §3, 1290-1294

Case

The general treasurer of a religious institute calls the office of the vicar for religious. She advises the vicar that the superior general has decided to sell a large novitiate in one of the provinces of the institute in the United States. The superior knows she must fulfill some canonical obligations and inquires as to what these are prior to selling the property.

QUESTIONS PERTINENT TO THE CASE

1. Is this an institute of diocesan right or an institute of pontifical right?
2. Is the generalate located in the diocese where the property is being sold?
3. If not, in what diocese is the novitiate located?
4. What led to the decision to sell the novitiate?
5. Has the religious institute any other use for this property?
6. Has the superior general followed the constitutions; is she the competent authority to give the written permission?
7. Does the superior general need and did she obtain the consent of the council?
8. Were there two appraisals of the property; what were these amounts?
9. Is the superior general aware of any other religious institute that may be interested in purchasing the property?
10. Is the diocesan bishop of the diocese where the property is located interested in purchasing it?
11. Has the superior general and her council obeyed all civil laws requiring the conveyance of property in that city or state?
12. What does the religious institute plan to do with the money received from the sale of   the property?

THE LAW

Can. 638 §3. For the validity of alienation and of any other affair in which the patrimonial condition of a juridic person can worsen, the written permission of the competent superior with the consent of the council is required. Nevertheless, if it concerns an affair which exceeds the amount defined by the Holy See for each region, or things given to the Church by vow, or things precious for artistic or historical reasons, the permission of the Holy See itself is also required.

§4. For the autonomous monasteries mentioned in can. 615 and for institutes of diocesan right, it is also necessary to have the written consent of the local ordinary.

COMMENTARY

It is important to know if the institute is of pontifical or diocesan right. If the institute is of diocesan right, she would need the written consent of the bishop of the diocese in which the generalate is located before alienating the property (c. 638 §4). In addition to the norms prescribed in the universal law and the proper law of the institute, the praxis of the CICLSAL is that all religious institutes need to have the *nihil obstat* of the diocesan bishop of the place where the property to be alienated is located. This is not a consent, but simply the bishop's statement that he has no objection to the sale of the ecclesiastical property.

There needs to be a just cause (*iusta causa)* for selling the property (c. 1293 §1, 1°). The fact that it is vacant or no longer necessary and the need for money to finance apostolic works or the retirement needs of the members would be sufficient. Having determined the just cause, CICLSAL requires at least one appraisal of the property (c. 1293 §1, 2°). This is to be certain that the property is sold for a fair price and the institute is not cheated in the transaction. There may be understandable differences in if there are two appraisals, as different companies take different approaches in estimating the value of property. If the appraisal is over five million dollars, the approval of the CICLSAL is required (c. 1292 §2, Prot. n. AG 126-2/03). It is important when petitioning CICLSAL to request to sell for the lower appraisal, since the amount requested will be on the rescript. A religious institute can sell the property for more than that amount, but could not sell it for less than the amount stated on the rescript from Rome.

The competent superior is obliged to obtain the consent of the council (cc. 638 §3, 1292 §1). This is most important, as it is for the validity of the sale or property. It requires a clear reading of the constitutions of the institute to see if the major superior is the general superior (supreme moderator) or the provincial superior. If there are four councilors, the major superior would need the consent of at least three of the councilors in order to sell the property (c. 127 §1). The superior and council should be careful to comply with all civil regulations regarding the transaction. It would be important, too, to honor the intention of donors who have given generously to the property. If people have given generous sums for the religious formation of young women in the institute, the monies should be used for initial or ongoing formation in the institute. Otherwise, the money received from the sale should be used for one of the four purposes for which ecclesiastical goods are employed: 1) divine worship, 2) care of the ministers, 3) apostolic works, and 4) charity (c. 1294 §2; 1254 §2).

Apart from the canonical and civil proceedings, it would be well pastorally to inform the membership of the sale and the reasons, particularly if the property holds sentimental value for them. Helping them understand the costs of maintaining the property, the liability of taxation if not used for apostolic purposes, and the need for the money from the sale for continued formation, other works, or the retirement fund will help to educate the members and gain their support for the administration in this often painful proceeding.

HELPFUL REFERENCES

- DePaolis, Velasio, C.S. "Temporal Goods of the Church in the New Code, With Particular Reference to Institutes of Consecrated Life." *The Jurist* 43:2 (1983) 343-360.

- Gallagher, Clarence. "Temporal Administration in the New Code." *The Way Supplement* 50 (Summer 1984) 71-80.

- Hite, Jordan F. "Property Issues for Religious." *CLSA Proceedings of the Forty-eighth Annual Convention* (October 13-16, 1986) 139-142.

- Kennedy, Robert T. "McGrath, Maida, Michiels: Introduction to a Study of the Canonical and Civil Law Status of Church-Related Institutions in the United States." *The Jurist* 50:2 (1990) 351-401.

- Maida, Adam J. and Nicholas P. Cafardi. *Church Property, Church Finances, and Church-Related Corporations - A Canon Law Handbook.* St. Louis: US CHA, 1984.

- Morrisey, Francis G. "The Alienation of Temporal Goods in Contemporary Practice." *Studia canonica* 29/2 (1995) 293-316.

- _____. "The Conveyance of Ecclesiastical Goods." *CLSA Proceedings of the Thirty-eighth Annual Convention* (1976) 123-137.

- _____. "Ordinary and Extraordinary Administration." *The Jurist* 48 (1988) 709-726.

RECOMMENDED LETTER

Most Rev. Archbishop Franc Rodé
Congregation for Institutes of Consecrated Life
    and Societies of Apostolic Life
Piazza Pio XII, 3
00193 Rome, Italy

Dear Archbishop Rodé,

   I, Sister _____, Superior General of _____, a religious institute of pontifical right located in the Diocese of _____,request to alienate our property located in the Diocese of _____. We have fulfilled the requirements of canon law and the proper law of our institute:

1. There is a just cause for the sale: scarcity of members and non-use of the building;
2. Two appraisals estimate the value of the property at approximately eight million dollars.
3. The council has given consent as required in canon law (c. 638 §3) and in our Constitutions (norm____).
4. The diocesan bishop of the diocese where the property is located has given his *nihil obstat* (see attached letter).
5. All requirements of civil law have been fulfilled concerning the sale of the property.
6. The proceeds of the sale will be used for thos purposes required in canon law, especially for our apostolate of health care.

   Thank you, Archbishop Rodé, for the time and concern you give this petition. Be assured of our prayer for you and your staff in your pastoral service to those under your care.

                    Gratefully yours,

                    _____
                    General Superior

PERMISSION TO ALIENATE PROPERTY - RESCRIPT

Prot. n._____

Most Holy Father,

The Superior General of the *Congregation of the Sisters of* _____, whose Generalate is in the Diocese of _____, requests of Your Holiness permission
to alienate _____, Street (City), for approximately US$_____, in accord with the reasons presented.

_____

The Congregation for Institutes of Consecrated Life and Societies of Apostolic Life, after hearing the opinion of the Most Reverend Ordinary of _____, grants the request in conformity with the petition. The provisions relating to the validity and lawfulness of alienation, found in canons 638-639 and in the proper law, are to be observed.

All things to the contrary notwithstanding.

Vatican, _____

Case 25

Admission to the Novitiate with a
Dispensation from the Impediment of the Marriage Bond
Canons 642, 643 §1, 2°

Case

A woman in her fifties asks for an interview with the vocation director of a religious congregation. She advises the sister that she would like to enter the institute. She is married and has raised four children. During her marriage her husband proved unfaithful and drank to excess; therefore, she separated from him. She has been an associate of this religious congregation and is very attracted to its spirituality and apostolate of social service. When her children were in high school, she took courses and earned a degree in social service.

QUESTIONS PERTINENT TO THE CASE

1. Does the woman have any other motives other than attraction to the spirit and apostolic work of the institute?
2. Did the marriage gradually breakdown, or was it doomed from the beginning?
3. Does the woman believe she contributed in any way to her husband's extra-marital affairs and excessive drinking?
4. Does she harbor any anger towards her husband's infidelity and intemperance?
5. How old are the children, and what are each of them presently doing?
6. Did she or her husband file for divorce; has he attempted another marriage?
7. Was their separation permanent in accord with the Code of Canon Law, or was it a decision she made due to his lifestyle?
8. Has she confided in anyone about her decision to enter religious life?
9. What are the attitudes of her children towards this decision?
10. Has she addressed this vocation with a confessor or spiritual director?
11. How is she preparing to enter religious life. Does she pray; go to Mass; receive spiritual direction?
12. Is the woman in good health, spiritually, emotionally, physically?
13. Is she friendly with any particular sister in the institute; has sister assisted her in describing the life she will live as a religious?

Can. 642 With vigilant care, superiors are only to admit those who, besides the required age, have the health, suitable character, and sufficient qualities of maturity to embrace the proper life of the institute. This health, character, and maturity are to be verified even by using experts, if necessary, without prejudice to the prescript of can. 220.

Can. 643 §1. The following are admitted to the novitiate invalidly:
   2° a spouse, while the marriage continues to exist;

COMMENTARY

It would be important to get a sense of what is attracting the woman to religious life. Is she despondent over her husband's infidelity to the marriage vow and unconsciously choosing religious life as a way to "show him." Important, too, is the history of the marriage. Were the husband's drinking and extra-marital affairs a reaction to any stress or tension in the union? Did he feel betrayed by her in the relationship; does she think she contributed in any way to the breakdown of the marriage? It should be remembered that this person has to meet the same requirements as any other applicant. The questions regarding the marriage are asked to determine if the women had culpability in the its breakdown. Religious life, like marriage, demands a commitment of persons to persons; it is a communal way of life in which husband and wife communicate Christ to each other and their children.

It would be well to know if there has been a divorce. While the marriage continues to endure in the eyes of the Church, it may well have lost legal effects in the civil court through divorce. The children's welfare is a grave consideration. What are their ages, and are they capable of fending for themselves. Are they well, and do any of them depend on their parents? What are their reactions to her decision? They may resent her decision, particularly if religious life would preclude visits from her. It would not be possible to admit someone who would still have the responsibilities of child rearing. Have all financial responsibilities been resolved? Are there other members of the family, i.e., mother, father, mother-in-law, father-in-law, who may depend on this woman for support. Are there an outstanding debts for which she is responsible?

It is also important to gain some insight into the spiritual life of the woman. Has this sadness in married life strengthened her or left her depressed? Does she pray, go to Mass frequently, attend lectures, go for spiritual direction, participate in any parish functions? What is her role and activity as an associate of the religious congregation? Is she familiar with one or more of the religious? Has she advised anyone of them of her decision? Does she realize from working with the sisters that she will have to give up some of the freedom and independence she enjoys to live communal life and the evangelical counsels.

If the vocation director is satisfied with the responses of the woman to her inquiries, she should advise her to approach the appropriate marriage tribunal to see if there is possibility of an annulment of the marriage. If the canonists advise her that there are not sufficient grounds for an annulment, but the major superior of the institute is willing to admit her to the novitiate, the vocation director or a canonist can recommend that the woman petition CICLSAL for a dispensation from the impediment of an existing marriage bond in order to enter the novitiate.

In assisting the woman with this procedure, it is important that time be taken to explain to her what she is petitioning. She must understand that she is asking for a dispensation from the impediment of an existing marriage bond, not from her marriage bond. If she leaves the religious institute or is dismissed, she will still be bound by the bond of marriage. If there is no decree of divorce, the applicant should file for divorce; otherwise, she is still bound civilly to her husband. It would be possible that there would be a civil basis for her husband to reclaim marital rights. CICLSAL requires a decree of permanent separation granted by the diocesan bishop of the competent tribunal from the spouse petitioning for a dispensation from the impediment of the marriage bond. This is to preclude the possibility of the husband demanding to resume marital life in the Church after she enters religious life. Included also with her petition would be copies of the marriage certificate and baptismal certificates of the petitioner, spouse, and children. If the husband has remarried, include a copy of his marriage license or a statement that he has no intention to resume marital rights with the applicant. If there is a decree of divorce, a copy of that decree should be included also. Finally, a statement from the major superior of the religious institute indicating her willingness to admit the petitioner to the novitiate should accompany the applicant's petition.

HELPFUL REFERENCES

- McDermott, Rose. "Admission to the Novitiate Canon 643 §1, 2° - Impediment of Existing Marriage Bond." *Bulletin on Issues of Religious Law* 7 (Spring 1991) 7-8.

The following is a copy of the Decree of Permanent Ecclesiastical Separation sent from an Archdiocese where the marriage took place. This would be included with the petitioner's letter and the supporting statement of the major superior willing to admit her to the novitiate.

Prot. n. _____

Decree of Permanent Ecclesiastical Separation

After a full oral contentious process, it is hereby decreed that _____ is granted a Permanent Ecclesiastical Separation from her husband, _____, on the basis of the following:

1. She was not the cause of the breakup of the marriage.
2. She was willing to accept him back and resume marital cohabitation.
3. _____sought and received a civil divorce on _____ .
4. _____ entered a civil marriage with _____ on _____(if husband attempted
   marriage) .
5. On _____, _____ submitted a petition for Permanent Ecclesiastical Separation.
6. _____ was sent this petition and, at no stage of the process, cooperated in any way. To protect his rights, _____ was informed that a procurator was appointed. He did not object.
7. Witnesses were heard.
8. No scandal is involved in granting this request.
9 The Promotor of Justice had no objection.
10. A formal hearing was held on _____ . Again, _____ did not cooperate.
11. The decision granting the Permanent Ecclesiastical Separation was sent to
    _____,
    giving him 15 days to appeal. As in the past, he has not contacted this Tribunal.

_____
Vicar Judicialis
Given at the Hall of the Tribunal

_____
_____

Congregation
for Institutes of Consecrated Life
and Societies of Apostolic Life

Prot. n. _____

Most Holy Father,

Mrs. _____, restricted by the bond of matrimony, implores Your Holiness for the necessary dispensation from the impediment in accord with canon 643 §1, 2° in the Code of Canon Law, so that the bond will not prevent her valid entrance into the novitiate of the Congregation of the Sisters of _____, archdiocese _____,
Latin Rite for the reasons given.

And God, etc.

By virtue of the special faculty given by the Supreme Pontiff, the Congregation for Institutes of Consecrated Life and Societies of Apostolic Life, having heard the petition, and in accord with the deliberations of the Congresso held _____, benignly grants the indult of dispensation from the above impediment, according to the request, everything else in the law being observed.

Anything contrary to the above does not stand.
Give in Rome, _____

_____
Secretary

_____
Undersecretary

Case 26

Special Feast Day for Perpetual Profession
Canons 655, 657

Case

A *novice director calls for the advice of a canonist regarding the date for the perpetual profession of three brothers. These religious made first profession on May 2ⁿᵈ and have renewed their vows annually on that date for the past three years. However, the customary date for final profession in the institute has been August 15ᵗʰ, the Assumption of the Blessed Virgin Mary. The director notes that the time of temporary profession expire on May 2ⁿᵈ, but the date set for perpetual profession is August 15ᵗʰ. How should the canonist advise the novice director?*

QUESTIONS PERTINENT TO THE CASE

1. Are the director of novices and other formation personnel satisfied with these religious in
   temporary profession and willing to recommend them for perpetual profession?
2. Has the major superior and council addressed the admission of the brothers to perpetual profession?
3. Do the religious seem happy and acclimated in their religious vocation?
4. Are the brothers willing to be admitted to final profession?
5. What are the provision in the proper law for both temporary and perpetual profession?

THE LAW

> Can. 655 Temporary profession is to be made for a period defined in proper law; it is not to be less than three years nor longer than six.

> Can. 657 §1. When the period for which profession was made has elapsed, a religious who freely petitions and is judged suitable is to be admitted to renewal of profession or to perpetual profession; otherwise, the religious is to depart.

131

§2. If it seems opportune, however, the competent superior can extend the period of temporary profession according to proper law, but in such a way that the total period in which the member is bound by temporary vows does not exceed nine years.

§3. Perpetual profession can be anticipated for a just cause, but not by more than three months.

COMMENTARY

The former code was rather strict regarding the exact time for renewing temporary profession, since a person could not remain in religious life without vows. However, since the Second Vatican Council there seems to be more of an emphasis on the intention of the person to make a total gift of self in religious profession. While the law provides for a period of temporary profession that is to last for no less than three years nor longer than six, the intent of the person professing vows should be a perpetual total gift of self to the Lord in response to his or her vocation. Even when the time of temporary profession has elapsed, there remains the intention of the person to live religious life perpetually. This theology of religious profession can be seen in individual responses of the CICLSAL to such questions put before that dicastery.

Today, many canonists are of the opinion that the intention of these religious to persevere and make perpetual profession in the institute suffices, even if their temporary profession expires on May 2nd, before they make perpetual profession on August 15th. This opinion seems well founded, because a religious who would make temporary profession without the intention of persevering in his or her vocation, and the determination to depart when things do not suit him or her, would profess invalidly. One could make an analogy to the exclusion of permanence in the sacrament of marriage (c. 1096 §1). On the other hand, if the member has sincerely tried to live the vocation, but discerned after prayer and spiritual direction that it was not his or her vocation, the expiration of temporary profession affords the religious a time to depart having fulfilled the time of the profession.

To avoid scruples or worry, the major superior could plan a small service in the oratory of the provincialate in which the brothers renewed their temporary vows on May 2nd until August 15th, and he would receive them in the name of the institute. Or the same superior could delegate the director of the temporary professed to do the same. However, before planning this renewal of temporary vows, the major superior should be well informed that each of the brothers is happy in his vocation and has petitioned for perpetual profession in accord with the proper law of the institute. Also, he should be certain that he and the council members have no reservations about admitting the brothers to perpetual profession in the institute on August 15th, based on the recommendations of the formation personnel and in accord with the proper law of the institute (cc. 657 §1, 658 2°).

If one of the brothers is not happy in his vocation or is judged unsuitable by the competent authority, it would be better early in May to assist him in departing the institute. He should receive the spiritual, psychological, and material help necessary to depart the institute in peace and resume the lay state (cc. 657 §1, 689 §1).

The following is an unofficial translation of a rescript from CICLSAL regarding this issue:

> Prot. n. _____
> Vatican, July 15, 2003
>
> I am answering your request for a *sanatio* concerning the irregular situation of the scholastic who remained without vows from February 18, 2002 until September 2002.
> I will say, Fr. Procurator, that the situation is in fact irregular; however, it implies no invalidity that would demand a *sanatio*. It will suffice that the superiors keep it in mind when the time comes to admit said scholastic to the perpetual vows. Religious vows are theologically perpetual right from the first temporary profession. Their temporary character refers only to some juridical effects, e.g., the possibility (for the candidate) not to be admitted to renew, or the freedom (of the candidate) to leave upon expiration without having to render account to anyone. The only causes of invalidity are those expressed in canons 656 and 658, or positively stated in the constitutions of the institute.
>
> _____
> Undersecretary
>
> Rev. _____
> Procurator General
> Rome

HELPFUL REFERENCES

- Castellano Cervera, Jesus. "Directives on Formation in Religious Institutes Some suggestions for a first reading of the Document *Potissimum Institutioni.*" *UISG Bulletin* 84 (1990) 32-51.

- CICLSAL. Directives, *Potissimum Institutioni,* February 2, 1990, *AAS* 82 (1990) 470-532. English translation in *Origins* 19 (1990) 677, 679-699.

- Futrell, John C., S.J. "The Dynamics of Religious Formation Some Principles that Apply to Growth in All Cultures." *Human Development* 2/4 (Winter 1981) 137-141.

- Hill, Richard A. "Denial of Profession." *Review for Religious* 47 (1988) 934-939.

Case 27

Unlawful Absence and Dismissal from the Institute
Canons 665 §2, 696 §1

Case

A major superior advises a canonist that one of their members walked out of her apostolate and never returned to the local house of the institute. The superior was advised by the natural sister of the religious that she is safe, but wants no contact with the institute. What canonical advice should the canonist offer the superior who is not certain how to address the situation?

QUESTIONS PERTINENT TO THE CASE

1. What kind of institute is concerned: one of diocesan or pontifical right?
2. Is the religious in perpetual profession; how long has she been in the institute?
3. Is sister in good health; had anything been upsetting her prior to her departure?
4. Is the superior aware of any difficulties in the workplace of the religious or in the local house that may have contributed to the abrupt departure?
5. Were the sisters who lived with sister aware of any issues that may have caused this precipitous act?
6. Was sister anxious about any change in her work or residence?
7. Is the superior aware of any family problem that may have prompted sister to depart so abruptly?
8. Has the sister of the religious offered any further information, other than the assurance of sister's safety?
9. Would it be possible to procure an address from the sister?
10. Has the superior attempted any intervention with the religious either personally or through her sister?

THE LAW

> Can. 665 §2. A member who is absent from a religious house illegitimately with the intention of withdrawing from the power of the superiors is to be sought out solicitously by them and is to be helped to return to and persevere in his or her vocation.

135

Can. 696 §1. A member can also be dismissed for other causes provided that they are grave, external, imputable, and juridically proven such as habitual neglect of the obligations of consecrated life; repeated violations of the sacred bonds; stubborn upholding or diffusion of doctrines condemned by the magisterium of the Church; public adherence to ideologies infected by materialism or atheism; the illegitimate absence mentioned in can. 665, §2, lasting six months; other causes of similar gravity which the proper law of the institute may determine.

COMMENTARY

The good news here is that the sister is safe and seemingly well; however, the bad news is that she willed to walk out of her ministry and failed to return to her religious house without notifying anyone. It may be important for the major superior (the provincial superior if there is a provincial level of governance in the institute) to know if there had been any issue or situation either in the local house or in sister's apostolic work that caused her precipitous act. The major superior should talk with the members of the local community to determine if sister has been upset about anything recently. On the other hand, the abrupt departure may come as no surprise to anyone, given the behavioral problems of the sister in question. At times, troubled members refuse counseling or assistance offered by the competent superiors of the institute.

After attempting to determine the cause for the abrupt departure of the sister, the major superior should try to persuade sister's sibling that it is in the latter's best interests for the superior to be in contact with her and assist her in whatever is bothering her. The superior should try to help the sibling understand the concern of the institute for one of its members and the responsibility of the superior to assist the religious at this troubled time. Often relatives are aware of erratic behavior in a brother or sister in religious life and can be persuaded to assist the proper authorities to address the situation.

If the major superior is able to obtain an address, she could make a decision to write a letter or make a personal visit to sister. Sometimes a non-threatening visit to show concern and to ask if the religious has what she needs may lead the religious to realize the concern of her institute and that she is not alone in facing any difficulty. Sometimes it is well to permit a few days to pass until the emotion cools down, and the religious is able to hear the concern of the superior.

After the major superior gains the trust of the religious, she should calmly advise her that, because she left so abruptly, she is in an irregular canonical status or an illegitimate absence from the institute (c. 665 §3). She should gently explain that there is a right way to seek temporary or permanent separation from the institute without simply walking out on one's responsibilities. If the sister has calmed down and admits to a vocational problem, the major superior can suggest that she request a period of exclaustration in order to examine her life as a religious (c. 686 §1). After careful discernment and spiritual direction while on

136

exclaustration, she may choose to petition for an indult of permanent separation (c. 691).

If the member refuses to see the major superior or does not respond to her registered mail explaining her situation and inviting her to seek an appointment, the major superior must wait six months before hearing the council and issuing the first canonical warning (c. 696 §1, 697). The canonical warning must contain the following: 1) what the religious did to merit the warning; 2) what she must do to remedy the problem; 3) she has a right to defend herself; 4) the time within which she must respond (at least fifteen days); and 5) her failure to respond and resolve the situation will result in a second canonical warning and dismissal from the religious institute (c. 697, 2 °). It may be wise to suggest that the sister seek canonical advice.

The second warning is relatively simple, since only the date of the warning and the date within which the superior expects to hear from the religious change. Everything else is the same: what the religious did, her obligation to remedy the situation, her right to defend herself to the provincial superior or the general superior (c. 698). It is important not to add other grounds than the grave cause presented in the first warning. If the sister offered an unacceptable or insufficient excuse, the second warning should state the same. If the second warning is in vain, the major superior sends all of the acts, signed personally and by a notary, along with any signed response or defense of the member (c. 697, 3°) to the general superior.

The general superior and the council (four members for validity) proceed collegially to consider the case: proofs, arguments, the defense of the member. If, through a secret collegial vote a decision is reached to dismiss the member, the supreme moderator issues a decree of dismissal containing for validity the reasons in law and in fact for the dismissal and the right of the religious to recourse within ten days from receiving notification (c. 699 §1, 700). However, the decree does not take effect until it is confirmed by the Apostolic See in the case an institute of pontifical right or the diocesan bishop of the house of assignment in the case of an institute of diocesan right. All of the acts of the case together with the decree must be submitted to the ecclesiastical authority. There is not need to repeat everything in the decree of dismissal in the letter to the ecclesiastical authority requesting confirmation. The acts should not be sent by e-mail, since they are official documents.

If the decree is confirmed by the competent ecclesiastical authority and the religious does not take recourse, the vows, rights, and obligation deriving from profession cease *ipso facto* (c. 791).If, on the other hand, she takes recourse, it must be made within ten days from receiving the notification of the dismissal. The recourse has suspensive effect until CICLSAL communicates its decision (c. 700). In either case, the sister should be treated with equity and charity at her dismissal in accord with the provisions of canon 702 §2.

HELPFUL REFERENCES

- Hill, Richard A. "Clarification of Dismissal: Canon 700." *Review for Religious* 46 (1987) 782-786.

- Holland, Sharon. "Chapter VI: Separation of Members from the Institute (cc. 684-704) 851-873 in *New Commentary on the Code of Canon Law*. Edited by John P. Beal et al. Washington, D.C.: CLSA, 2000.

- McDonough, Elizabeth. "The Troubling Religious: Further Considerations." *Review for Religious* (1990) 618-624.

SAMPLE

CANONICAL WARNING

Dear Sister _____

On (date)_____ you abruptly left your apostolic assignment and failed to return to your local community. I met with you on (date)_____ and advised you that you are unlawfully absent from our religious institute. Because you did not return as I requested, I sent two registered letters on (date)_____ and (date)_____that were returned to me unopened. Despite these efforts on my part, you remain in an irregular canonical state.

Because you are now six months unlawfully absent from our institute, I, regrettably, send you this first canonical warning advising you of your irregular canonical status and your obligation to meet with me on _____ or to call and make an appointment (phone #)_____ at a mutually agreeable time in order to discuss you return to our religious institute. Your failure to cooperate in this manner within thirty days (date)_____ will result in a second canonical warning and dismissal from our congregation. You have a right to defend yourself regarding this unlawful absence, and you may send your defense to me or to our general superior, _____ .

Be assured of my prayer during this time, and I hope that you contact me in order that I can assist you in returning to our congregation.

_____   _____
Date   Provincial Superior

PETITION FOR CONFIRMATION OF THE DECREE OF DISMISSAL

Most Rev. Archbishop Franc Rodé

Dear Archbishop Rodé

After several years of exhortation and effort, and having consulted _____, a canonist in the diocese of _____, I convoked the council on _____ . In accordance with canon 699 § 1 of the Code of Canon Law, the five of us proceeded in a collegial manner to study the facts of the case and by secret vote to decide on the dismissal of sister from our religious institute, the Sisters of _____ in the diocese of _____ .

According to canon 700, this decree requires for its validity the confirmation of your congregation. With the members of the general council whose signatures are below, I request that this decree be confirmed. Sister's continued illegitimate absence from our institute, her refusal to live common life and accept an assigned ministry in keeping with our congregation's constitutions and her vow of obedience have been a source of bad example to other members of our institute and place in serious questioning the essentials of our apostolic religious life. Sister has refused to seek and indult of departure from our congregation even after receiving sound canonical advice.

I enclose the documents of the dismissal process: a) copies of the two canonical warnings; b) a detailed summary of the administration's interactions with sister over a period of _____ years, c) a *curriculum vitae* for sister, and d) the decree of dismissal.

I deeply appreciate the concern, attention and time you afford this regrettable and grave matter.

Sincerely yours,

_____
General Superior
(Signatures of four councilors)

DECREE OF DISMISSAL

Sister _____

Dear Sister,

Since I received no response from you to the two canonical warnings issued on _____ and _____, I was left with no alternative than to convoke the council on _____ . After serious and detailed consideration of this administration's pleading with you over a period of _____ years, we proceeded through a secret collegial vote to dismiss you from our religious institute.

This collegial vote of the general council to dismiss you from our institute is based on a) your unwillingness to respond to either of the two canonical warnings addressing your illegitimate absence from the institute; b) your removal of yourself from the legitimate authority vested in the superiors and constitutions of the institute, and c) your refusal to return to communal life and accept an assigned apostolate according to our institute's constitutions.

This decision of the general council was confirmed by the Apostolic See on _____. Enclosed is a copy of the same. You have a right, sister, to take recourse against this dismissal within ten days of receiving this notification. I am sending this letter as I sent the canonical warnings by registered mail, and you can contact the following person in Rome:

(Give name, address, phone, fax, e-mail for CICLSAL)

Undoubtedly, sister, this is the most regrettable action I have had to take during my service as general superior of our institute. You continue in my prayer, as you strive to seek peace and the Lord's direction in your life.

Sincerely yours,

_____

General Superior

Case 28

Living Apart or Exclaustration from a *Sui Iuris* Monastery
Canons 665 §1, 667 §4, 686-687

Case

A nun calls a canonist from a health care facility where she is being treated for depression. She will be discharged in a month and is fearful of returning to the demands of community life in the monastery. She is concerned, too, about seeking employment beyond the monastery, as she has limited skills. She needs advice in approaching her major superior with these issues and canonical advice regarding the procedure for leaving the monastery.

QUESTIONS PERTINENT TO THE CASE

1. Is the monastery of pontifical or diocesan right; of papal or constitutional cloister?
2. Is it a *sui iuris* monastery as described in canon 615?
3. How many religious are in the monastery?
4. How old is the religious; is she in temporary or perpetual profession?
5. Does she know yet what the doctor will recommend at her departure from the hospital?
6. Will she be expected to have follow-up therapy or counseling?
7. What are sister's skills; what has she done in the monastery as a religious?
8. Has the nun described the fear of returning to the monastery to her therapist at the facility; has he or she given any practical suggestions?
9. Does her superior visit her in the facility; has she raised the issue of sister's return to the monastery; is she aware that sister is fearful of returning to the monastery?
10. Who recommended that she call a canonist, or did she initiate this on her own?

THE LAW

> Can. 665 §1. Observing common life, religious are to live in their own religious house and are not to be absent from it except with the permission

of their superior. If it concerns a lengthy absence from the house, however, the major superior, with the consent of the council and for a just cause, can permit a member to live outside a house of the institute, but not for more than a year, except for the purpose of caring for ill health, of studies, or of exercising an apostolate in the name of the institute.

Can. 667 §3. Monasteries of nuns which are ordered entirely to contemplative life must observe *papal* cloister, that is, cloister according to the norms given by the Apostolic See. Other monasteries of nuns are to observe a cloister adapted to their proper character and defined in the constitutions.

§4. For a just cause, a diocesan bishop has the faculty of entering the cloister of monasteries of nuns which are in his diocese and, for a grave cause and with the consent of the superior, of permitting others to be admitted to the cloister and the nuns to leave it for a truly necessary period of time.

Can. 686 §2. It is only for the Apostolic See to grant an indult of exclaustration for nuns.

Can. 687. An exclaustrated member is considered freed from the obligations which cannot be reconciled with the new condition of his or her life, yet remains dependent upon and under the care of superiors and also of the local ordinary, especially if the member is a cleric. The member can wear the habit of the institute unless the indult determines otherwise. Nevertheless, the member lacks active and passive voice.

COMMENTARY

The canonist should visit the nun in the health care facility to learn of her religious life experience and the nature of her monastery. It would be important to learn if sister has discussed this possible decision of leaving the monastery with anyone else, particularly her major superior or therapist. It may be that one of them advised her to seek the advice of a canonist. The difficulties of religious departing an intense cloistered life can often be more problematic, since they are often unprepared to meet the challenges of secular life.

The canonist should learn the canonical status of the nun. If she is in temporary vows, it may be that the major superior has been advised by the novice director or formation personnel that the particular religious lifestyle is too demanding for her. Or it may be that she has come to this decision through therapy in the health care facility. Her monastery would assist her in returning to the life of a lay person and meeting its challenges. Depending on the amount of time the religious has lived in the monastery, her need, and the capability of the monastery, there will most likely be a policy in place addressing monetary assistance as she voluntarily departs or is excluded from further profession and asked to leave the monastery. The canonist should gently explain this to the nun and advise her to talk with her major superior. Often, superiors are willing to permit the member to live in the religious house until he or she secures gainful employment and living quarters.

If, on the other hand, the nun has spent a number of years in the monastery and is a religious in perpetual profession, the onus is greater on the monastery to provide for her needs at this time. It would be important for the canonist to determine what the recommendation of the therapist is for the nun. It may be that she needs the support of the community as she recovers from depression, or it may be that the therapist is recommending a time away from the life of the cloister. At times it is not in the best interests of a person plagued by depression to live alone, so here the advice of the therapist is important.

If, however, the therapist is recommending time away from the monastery, it may be well to recommend that the nun petition for permission to live apart from the monastery for reasons of ill health in accord with canon 665 §1. If the major superior secures the consent of the council, she would need to follow the proper law according to whether the monastery has provisions for papal or constitutional cloister. If the *sui iuris* monastery has papal cloister, the practice of CICLSAL in accord with *Verbi Sponsa* 17 is that the major superior can give whatever time is needed for reasons of health. It may be wise initially for the nun to petition for a one year period, since this leaves time for evaluation before an extension of the time is given.

If, during the canonist's visit, the nun advises that she has a vocation problem and is seriously planning to depart the monastery definitively, the canonist would advise the nun to petition for an indult of exclaustration which would be granted by CICLSAL. She should understand that this will be a significant challenge for her, since she has lived a cloistered life for so long. The canonist should be willing to meet with her major superior regarding this request. Issues such as ongoing counseling, health care, and monetary assistance would be considerations. It may be well not to depart the monastery until the nun has secured perhaps part time employment initially and a place to live. If the bouts with depression seem to improve as the nun lives on her own, it may be that the major superior and council would be willing to assist her in procuring some proficiency, e.g., nursing or computer skills that would assist her in securing a full time position. With full time work, she may have the assurance of health benefits and retirement.

A decision like this should not be handled hastily, and the canonists should know the facts above before giving advice. The nun should be informed as to the rights and obligations of one on exclaustration (c. 687) and realize she remains under the care of her major superior during that time. The canonist should advise that she remain on exclaustration until she is sufficiently well and adjusted to procure an indult of definitive departure from the monastery in accord with canon 691. All of this depends of course on her general health, age, and her ability to provide for herself apart from the more secure life of the monastery.

145

- CICLSAL Instruction, *Verbi Sponsa,* May 13, 1999.
  The document can be procured on line by visiting:
  http://www.vatican.va/roman_curia/congreg...scrlife.doc_13051999_verbi-sponsa_en.html.

- McDonough, Elizabeth. "Exclaustration: Canonical Categories and Current Practice." *The Jurist* 49/2 (1989) 568-606.

- Ruessmann, Madeleine. "Aspects of Exclaustration." *Periodica* 84/II (1995) 237-266.

- Torres, Jesus. "Procedure for the Exclaustration of a Religious." *Consecrated Life* 18/1 (1993) 47-73.

Case 29

Act of Cession and Act of Renunciation
Canon 668

Case

A forty-three year old woman approaches a canonist at the recommendation of the abbess of a monastery. The woman has secured an annulment and wishes to enter the contemplative monastery. In the course of the conversation she advises the canonist that she has property in the diocese, substantial savings, and a number of certificates of deposit. She would like to give her assets to the monastery, but the abbess is hesitant and sent her to the canonist. What advice should the canonist give this woman?

QUESTIONS PERTINENT TO THE CASE

1. What is the canonical status of the monastery; is it *sui iuris* with one major superior, or is it joined to other monasteries subject to a major superior besides its own superior?
2. Did the abbess send the canonist a copy of the *Rule* or *Constitutions* of the monastery?
3. Is the woman a Catholic; what is the condition of her health?
4. What is her general background: early family life, education, work experience, faith life?
5. How long was she married; why did the marriage terminate, and what were the grounds for which the annulment was given?
6. Does she have any children by the marriage; how old are they; are they independent?
8. Are her parents living; does she have siblings or relatives dependent on her?
9. Does she have any contact with her former husband; which of them petitioned for the   annulment?
10. Why is she choosing to enter the contemplative religious life; does she know anything about this kind of religious life, about the spirituality of the monastery she has chosen?
11. Does the abbess of the monastery have other hesitancies other than the temporal

goods of the woman?

12. Why does she want to give her assets to the monastery at this time?

THE LAW

Can. 668 §1.   Before first profession, members are to cede the administration of their goods to whomever they prefer and, unless the constitutions state otherwise, are to make disposition freely for their use and revenue. Moreover, at least before perpetual profession, they are to make a will which is to be valid also in civil law.

§2.   To change these dispositions for a just cause and to place any act regarding temporal goods, they need the permission of the superior competent according to the norm of proper law.

§3.   Whatever a religious acquires through personal effort or by reason of the institute, the religious acquires for the institute. Whatever accrues to a religious in any way by reason of pension, subsidy, or insurance is acquired for the institute unless proper law states otherwise.

§4.   A person who must renounce full his or her goods due to the nature of the institute is to make that renunciation before perpetual profession in a form valid, as far as possible, even in civil law; it is to take effect from the day of profession. A perpetually professed religious who wishes to renounce his or her goods either partially or totally according to the norm of proper law and with the permission of the supreme moderator is to do the same.

§5.   A professed religious who has renounced his or her goods fully due to the nature of the institute loses the capacity of acquiring and possessing and therefore invalidly   places acts contrary to the vow of poverty. Moreover, whatever accrues to the professed after renunciation belongs to the institute according to the norm of proper law.

COMMENTARY

First it would be important to have a sense of the kind of monastery the woman has chosen to enter. Is it one that has an external major superior in addition to the internal local superior or is it a *sui iuris* monastery with a major superior as described in canon 615? The canonist would be advised to request a copy of the *Rule* or proper law of the monastery so as to review its provisions for admission and the disposition of temporal goods before meeting with the woman.

The canonist should focus on the woman who has come for the meeting. Is she a Catholic? What is her the condition of her health, her general background and in particular the failed marriage? Does she have any children resultant from the marriage and what are their ages? All of these issues are important to determine if the woman has any impediments and possesses the qualities for admission to the novitiate of the monastery. While the canonist is not the authority to admit, he or she may note for the major superior an important factor that should be considered apart from the woman's temporal goods. If the canonist recognizes an impediment or a significant quality lacking, then it would be important to have the candidate report this to the major superior or request the woman to free the canonist to address the issue with the major superior of the monastery..

When the canonist has gained insight into the background of the woman and determines that there is a potential candidate for admission to the monastery, he or she could then begin to explain the provision of canon law regarding the vow of poverty in religious institutes (c. 668), and in particular in the monastery. It would be most important to advise the woman from the beginning that under no conditions should she divest herself of her personal goods at any time during the formation period until she is certain that she is prepared to petition for perpetual profession and the competent authority is willing to admit her to the same in the monastery.

Canon 668 can be explained to the woman in simple terms. In order for her to focus on her religious life, she is obliged before her first profession to cede or yield the administration of her goods to whomever she chooses and to decide what she wishes to do with their use and revenue (c. 668 §1). Often persons have monies invested with interest added to the principal. However, this woman would need someone to administer the property for her, and an account of what she decides to do should be kept in her file in the monastery.. It would be well if she has no relatives or a trustworthy person that the canonist suggest she seek the advice of a trustworthy financial advisor. The latter could certainly call the canonist to seek information regarding the obligations of religious life until the woman is ready for perpetual profession.

She should also be advised that if she decides to change these dispositions or the financial advisor advises the same, she needs to secure the permission of the major superior of the monastery. This is ordinarily given as long as the best interests of the woman are the consideration (c. 668 §2). Once she makes first profession, whatever she may acquire through personal effort as a religious is acquired for the monastery. In other words, if she has talent in sewing, music, writing, etc., the proceeds of whatever is sold would belong to the monastery by reason of her vow of poverty at religious profession (c. 668 §3). It should be repeated that if at any time she is not happy or believes that the vocation is not her calling, she can petition to leave the monastery. This is the reason why it is so important to avoid divesting her goods until there is reasonable certainty regarding her lifelong vocation a woman religious.

If she is happy in the monastery and the major superior judges her suitable in accord with the norms of the *Constitutions* of the monastery, she would be admitted to solemn profession. Before the perpetual profession, she would be obliged to renounce her temporal goods, i.e., giving them to whomever she pleases and make an act of renunciation that would be valid in civil law, if possible, to take place from the day of perpetual profession (c. 668 §4). This means that not only would she divest herself of what she presently owns, but she would lose the capacity of acquiring and possessing in the future and invalidly place acts contrary to the vow of poverty. Whatever temporal goods would come to her by way of patrimony or gift after the act of renunciation would belong to the institute according to its proper law (c. 668 §5).

The woman should be constantly made aware that the interest of the Church and the monastery is her vocation, not her temporal goods. Likewise, she has no assurance that she will persevere in the monastery or the competent authority will judge her suitable for admission to profession. Therefore, it is important that she make provision that her temporal goods are wisely and honestly administered until such time as her perpetual profession. At that time, she would renounce her goods in accord with the nature of the institute in a form valid, as far as possible, in civil law (c. 668 §4). With this renunciation she loses the capacity of acquiring and possessing temporal goods. Whatever comes to her following the renunciation belongs to the religious institute in accord with the norms of the proper law (c. 668 §5).

HELPFUL REFERENCES

- Hill, Richard A. "Financial Patrimony." *Review for Religious* 44 (1985) 140-144.

- _____ . "Patrimony Revisited." *Review for Religious* 49 (1990) 137-141.

- Mayer, Augustine. "Pensions of Religious" *Consecrated Life* 5/2 (1979) 204.

- McDermott, Rose. "Evangelical Poverty and the Vow in Religious Life." *Religious Life Review* 36 (November/December 1997) 357-367.

- Morrisey, Francis G. "The Vow of Poverty and Personal Patrimony." *CLSGB&I Newsletter* 72 (December 1987) 26-34.

- "Religious and Social Security." *Consecrated Life* 2/2 (1976) 170-173.

ACT OF CESSION AND PROVISION FOR USE AND REVENUE

I, _____, in the City of _____, State of
_____, in consideration of the laws of the Roman Catholic Church
concerning the administration of temporal goods, their use and revenue, for a
member of a religious institute as stated by the said Church in canon 668 of the
Code of Canon Law for the Latin Church:

First, do cede for the time that I shall be a member in temporal profession of the
Monastery of _____, the administration of my temporal goods to
_____ .

Second, I declare that during the same period of time the interest, rent, income,
annuities, royalties, bonus, etc. shall be disposed of or expended in the following
manner:

_____

_____

Third, I declare that if, for any reason, I shall refuse or be rejected admission to
perpetual profession in the Monastery, both the above-named cession of
administration of my real and personal property and the disposition of the use and
revenue of the property shall cease, terminate, and be null and void, as if it had
never been made.

Fourth, I declare that I shall never claim or demand directly or indirectly any
compensation, remuneration, annuity, or pension for the service I perform with or
for said Monastery during the time I spend there or for future considerations,
knowing that the laws of the Roman Catholic Church will not uphold or defend any
claim of any kind to wages or remuneration.

In witness whereof, I have subscribed my name this _____day of
_____ in the year of Our Lord, _____ .

_____   _____
Witness   Signed

SAMPLE

ACT OF RENUNCIATION

I, _____, of the Monastery of _____, having been admitted to Perpetual Profession in the same Monastery, give and transfer the ownership, to be effective upon the act of my profession, of all temporal goods and property which I now possess and which may come to me in the future in accord with the laws of the Church and the proper law of the Monastery for those being admitted to perpetual profession as follows:

_____

_____

In witness whereof, I have set my hand this _____ day of _____ in the year of Our Lord _____ .

_____   _____
Witness   Signed

_____
Notary Public

Case 30

Obligations of the Vow of Poverty in a Religious Institute
Canons 600, 607 §2, and 668

Case

A sister in a religious congregation is one of two siblings who has recently lost both parents. Since the father was rather wealthy, he left his possessions to his son (sister's brother) to provide for both the son and daughter in religious life. Sister's brother has provided her with a "gold credit card" and a monthly amount of cash. Likewise, he has informed her that whenever she wants anything: car, computer, cell phone, stereo, she need only purchase it or ask him, and he will see that she receives the desired item. The sister seems to think that this is fine, since the brother provides all she needs and her institute does not have these expenses. How would a canonist address this distorted sense of the vow of poverty?

QUESTIONS PERTINENT TO THE CASE

1. Is the institute of pontifical or diocesan right?
2. Since it is described as a religious "congregation," is an act of renunciation not required at perpetual profession?
3. How long is sister in the religious congregation; what is her status, temporary or perpetual profession?
4. How long has this arrangement been going on, and what has she requested and accepted from her brother?
5. Was any instruction given to sister at the time of her novitiate prior to temporary profession regarding the nature of the vow of poverty she would profess?
6. Did sister sign an act of cession; was she aware of the implications of that cession prior to her temporary profession?
7. Has any superior addressed this distorted sense of poverty, and what was sister's reaction to the intervention or correction?

Can. 600 The evangelical counsel of poverty in imitation of Christ who, although he was rich, was made poor for us, entails, besides a life which is poor in fact and in spirit and is to be led productively in moderation and foreign to earthly riches, a dependence and limitation in the use and disposition of goods according to the norm of the proper law of each institute.

Can. 607 §2. A religious institute is a society in which members, according to proper law, pronounce public vows, either perpetual or temporary which are to be renewed, however, when the period of time has elapsed and lead a life of brothers or sisters in common.

Can. 668 §1. Before first profession, members are to cede the administration of their goods to whomever they prefer and, unless the constitutions state otherwise, are to make disposition freely for their use and revenue. Moreover, at least before perpetual profession, they are to make a will which is to be valid also in civil law. §2. To change these dispositions for a just cause and to place any act regarding temporal goods, they need the permission of the superior competent according to the norm of proper law.
§3. Whatever a religious acquires through personal effort or by reason of the institute, the religious acquires for the institute. Whatever accrues to a religious in any way by reason of pension, subsidy, or insurance is acquired for the institute unless proper law states otherwise.
§4. A person who must renounce full his or her goods due to the nature of the institute is to make that renunciation before perpetual profession in a form valid, as far as possible, even in civil law; it is to take effect from the day of profession. A perpetually professed religious who wishes to renounce his or her goods either partially or totally according to the norm of proper law and with the permission of the supreme moderator is to do the same.
§5. A professed religious who has renounced his or her goods fully due to the nature of the institute loses the capacity of acquiring and possessing and therefore invalidly places acts contrary to the vow of poverty. Moreover, whatever accrues to the professed after renunciation belongs to the institute according to the norm of proper law.

COMMENTARY

It may be that this sister is inexperienced, recently professed, and compensated for the recent death of her parents with the attention of her brother for her "needs". If she is a seasoned religious, one could well inquire about her formation in religious life and her understanding of the public vow of poverty she professed in accord with canon law and the proper law of the institute (c. 654).

Religious commit themselves to common life, i.e., common housing, food, clothing, and other necessities in accord with the proper law of the institute. They vow a life in imitation of Christ, poor in fact and in spirit, a life of labor in moderation, and a life of dependence and limitation in the use and disposition of goods according to the proper law of their institutes (c. 600). The religious institute is obliged by canon law to supply the member with all those things which are necessary to achieve the purpose of her vocation in accord with the norm of the constitutions (c. 670).

Prior to her first profession, sister was to sign an act of cession whereby she gave the administration of her temporal goods to whomever she wished. Likewise, she was to dispose of the use and revenue of the same (c. 668 §1). In order to change the act of cession or to place an act regarding her temporal goods, the sister would need the permission of the competent superior in accord with the proper law of her institute. (c. 668 §2). Sister's major superior should remind her of the act of cession she made and ask her if the content of the cession needed to be addressed in light of the recent death of her parents.

It should be further explained to sister by the major superior that her vocation to religious life is lived in common with the other members of the institute and in dependence on the institute for what is necessary to live out her vocation. If she wants to contribute to her religious institute out of her personal patrimony administered by her brother, she would need to ask permission of the competent superior to do so. But that does not give license for her to have whatever she desires that would be incompatible with common life or unnecessary to carry out her vocation. Whatever she deems necessary for her to carry out her vocation should be requested of her religious institute in the person of the competent superior. Sister cannot simply ask her brother for whatever she believes she needs and live a life that is contrary to her vow of poverty and the common life of her sisters in community.

The major superior should exercise patience with the religious, for it may be that the vow of poverty was never thoroughly explained to her. As noted above, she may be going through a period of crisis with the death of her parents, and her brother's attention consoles her at this time. Nevertheless, she should be made aware that such a distorted sense of poverty is contrary to the common life she agreed to live, a violation of the vow of poverty she professed, a poor witness of religious life to her brother, and a possible temptation to other members to do likewise with their temporal goods.

HELPFUL REFERENCES

- McDermott, Rose. "Evangelical Poverty and the Vow in Religious Life." *Religious Life Review* 36 (November/December 1997) 357-367.

- McDonough, Elizabeth. "Poverty, Patrimony, and Nest Eggs." *Review for Religious* 50/4 (July/August 1991) 617-625.

- Morrisey, O.M.I., Francis G. "The Vow of Poverty and Personal Patrimony." *CLSGB&I Newsletter* 72 (1987) 26-34.

Case 31

Obligation of an Institute Towards its Members
Canons 670; 584; 616 §2, §4; 702 §2

Case

A woman in her late sixties appears in a parish. She has been inquiring about the possibilities for work and shelter. The matter is reported to the pastor, and he meets with the woman. She advises him that her religious community "folded" and that she must seek work and a place to live. The pastor reports the matter to the vicar for religious who hears the same story from the woman. The vicar decides to seek monetary assistance for the woman from the bishop, but first seeks the advice of a canonist.

QUESTIONS PERTINENT TO THE CASE

1. How long had she been in religious life; was she in perpetual profession?
2. What is the name of the religious institute; was it of diocesan or pontifical right?
3. What does the woman mean by the term "folded"?
4. How many religious were in the institute at that time it "folded"?
5. What happened to the rest of the members; did they merge with another institute; did they unite with other institutes, did they transfer; did they seek dispensation?
6. In what diocese was the institute; where was its generalate?
7. Did the woman have any options when the institute "folded"? Had she transferred to another institute; did she seek a dispensation from her religious vows?
8. Has she any rescript or other document to show her canonical status?
9. Was she given any financial assistance at all when the institute "folded"?
10. Does she have Social Security; did the institute have this provision for its members?

THE LAW

Can. 120 §1. A juridic person is perpetual by its nature; nevertheless, it is extinguished if it is legitimately suppressed by competent authority or has ceased to act for a hundred years.

§2. If even one of the members of a collegial juridic person survives, and the aggregate of persons (*universitas personarum*)has not ceased to exist according to its statutes, that member has the exercise of all the rights of the aggregate *(universitas)*.

Can. 584 The suppression of an institute pertains only to the Apostolic See; a decision regarding the temporal goods of the institute is also reserved to the Apostolic See.

Can. 616 §2. The suppression of the only house of an institute belongs to the Holy See, to which the decision regarding the goods in that case is also reserved.

§4. To suppress an autonomous monastery of nuns belongs to the Apostolic See, with due regard to the prescripts of the constitutions concerning its goods.

Can. 670 An institute must supply the members with all those things which are necessary to achieve the purpose of their vocation, according to the norm of the constitutions.

Canon 702 §1. Those who depart from a religious institute legitimately or have been dismissed from it legitimately can request nothing from the institute for any work done in it.

§2. Nevertheless, the institute is to observe equity and the charity of the gospel toward a member who is separated from it.

COMMENTARY

Two important issues must be resolved: 1) the canonical status of the "folded" institute, and 2) the canonical status of the woman. "Folded" is not a canonical term, and the canonist should investigate as to the past and present status of the institute. Was it a religious institute of diocesan or pontifical right? Was it suppressed by the Apostolic See (c. 584); or did it merge or unite with another institute or institutes (c. 582)? If the canonist discovers that the entity never matured to a religious institute of diocesan or pontifical right, then the laws for religious institutes do not apply. Since the woman would not be a religious, her needs would have to be addressed through the assistance provided for needy persons in the diocese.

If the institute did have canonical status and the religious decided due to lack of vocations and scarcity of members to gradually die out, to merge with another institute, or to unite with another institute or institutes, it has the obligation to provide for its members. In the case of gradual extinction, the members remain in the institute and their needs are addressed in accord with canon 670, as the administration of the institute provides for the gradual extinction of the institute. If the institute merged or united, its assets would be joined to the institute or institutes to which it united. However, it would still have to provide in some way for members who choose to transfer or depart the institute. If the institute had been suppressed by CICLSAL, the individual members would have been provided for in accord with canon 584.

The next issue to be resolved is the canonical status of this woman. Did she make perpetual profession in the religious institute? What decision did she make when the institute "folded"? Did she transfer to another institute or seek an indult of departure? These are the options that CICLSAL offers members of religious institutes when there is a decision for a merger or union. If she sought a transfer to another institute, she would not be admitted to perpetual profession in that institute until she completed at least three years of probation. If the woman transferred and was unhappy and decided to leave during the probationary period, or if she were asked to depart the institute, she has a right to return to the institute with which her original institute merged or united with other institutes to form. She has a right to be received by this institute or to seek an indult of departure and receive monetary assistance in accord with canon 702 §2.

If she decided to seek an indult of departure prior to the institute's merging or uniting with other institutes, she would have been provided some financial assistance in accord with the policy of the institute and equity and charity (c. 702 §2). Her indult of departure would have been processed through the initial institute before the merger or union.

The diocesan bishop of the diocese where she has been seeking employment and financial assistance is not the person responsible to provide for the woman. The canonist and the vicar for religious should thoroughly investigate the matter and see if the sister was treated with justice, equity, and charity and if she legitimately departed or was dismissed from the institute. If the members of the institute agreed to eventual extinction, all of them would have remained with the institute and been provided for in accord with canon 670. If she legitimately departed, she would have been given monetary assistance in accord with canon 702 §2.

It would seem highly unlikely that the temporal goods of the institute were distributed without concern for this woman. Ordinarily, administrations of institutes recognize their responsibilities in providing for the members whether they definitively depart, transfer, or move with the institute in the merger or union. So a thorough investigation is needed into the past and present canonical status of the "folded" institute and the past and present juridical status of this woman claiming to be a religious.

HELPFUL REFERENCES

- Euart, Sharon. "Religious Institutes and the Juridical Relationship of the Members to the Institute." *The Jurist* 51 (1991) 103-118.

- McDermott, Rose. "External and Internal Reconfiguration of Religious Institutes." *Commentarium Pro Religiosis et Missionariis* vol. 86/I-II: 57-81. See esp. 68-69.

- McDonough, Elizabeth. "The Protectionof Rights in Religious Institutes." *The Jurist* 46 (1986) 164-204.

- Welch, Madeline and Peter Campbell. "Provisions for Departing Members." *Bulletin on Issues of Religious Law* 12 (Fall 1996).

Case 32

Agreements for Religious in Apostolic Works
Canons 681-682

Case

    An archdiocese has contracts for religious in education in the parochial and secondary schools. At present, religious are applying for other apostolates such as directors of religious education, pastoral and social ministers in parishes, staff in diocesan offices, and prison ministry. The archbishop requests his canonist to draw up an agreement or contract between him and the major superiors of these institutes. What would be some provisions the canonist should consider in formulating the draft?

QUESTIONS PERTINENT TO THE CASE

1. Are the archbishop and the major superior satisfied with the contracts for education?
2. What are some of the essential elements in the school contracts?
3. In addition to the elements in canon 681, what other provisions are included in these school contracts?
4. Have any of the pastors drafted contracts for other ministries in their parishes in the absence of an archdiocesan one?
5. Has the canonist inquired as to contracts or agreements in the neighboring dioceses?
6. Has the canonist procured the latest statement of compensation for religious in the various dioceses of the United States published by National Association of Church Personnel Administrators?
7. Has the diocesan bishop constituted any of the apostolates as an "ecclesiastical office" in the canonical sense of the term?

THE LAW

    Can. 681 §1. Works which a diocesan bishop entrusts to religious are subject to the authority and direction of the same bishop, without prejudice to the right of religious superiors according to the norm of can. 678, §§2 and 3.

§2. In these cases, the diocesan bishop and the competent superior of the institute are to draw up a written agreement which, among other things, is to define expressly and accurately those things which pertain to the work to be accomplished, the members to be devoted to it, and economic matters.

Can. 682 §1. If it concerns conferring an ecclesiastical office in a diocese upon some religious, the diocesan bishop appoints the religious, with the competent superior making the presentation, or at least assenting to the appointment.

§2. A religious can be removed from the office entrusted to him or her at the discretion either of the entrusting authority after having informed the religious superior or of the superior after having informed the one entrusting; neither requires the consent of the other.

COMMENTARY

Canon 681 addresses "works entrusted to religious," commonly understood as those works which a bishop, pastor, or another person responsible for a public juridic person requests or invites religious to perform. They are distinct from "works proper to the institute" which are works included in the design of the founder or foundress with the approval and erection of the institute. Religious institutes carry on the "works proper" in various dioceses with the consent of the diocesan bishop (e.g., schools, hospitals, social service institutions). However "works entrusted" can be used in a more generic sense to include the "works proper" since the latter are the works the members are competent to perform. Suitable agreements or contracts agreeable to both the diocesan bishop representing the diocese and the major superior representing the religious institute should be signed by both indicating their acceptance of the agreement. (c. 681 §1). Since this is a work "entrusted" to the institute, the diocesan bishop has a canonist or legal advisor draw us such an agreement and present it to the major superior for his or her acceptance before it is signed by both.

The canon addresses a number of religious in a specific work, e.g. parish, social ministry, nursing home, school, etc. However, the same canon or canon 682 can be applied to a situation in which one religious is assigned by his or her major superior to a "work entrusted" to a religious. There are few ecclesiastical offices identified in the Code of Canon Law to which lay religious can be assigned. However, the contents of both canons should be considered and applied to an individual religious assigned or given permission by a major superior to accept a work not identified in the code as an ecclesiastical office in the diocesan curia or in some type of parish ministry. Some of the content to be included in the agreement or contract follows:

Canon 681 §2 calls for a description of the work to be done. An accurate and precise job description is important, since it protects the rights of the individual religious or community of religious performing the apostolate and the employer who expects that he/she or they will accomplish the same. If the apostolate requires more than one religious (parish, nursing home, social work facility), it is important to indicate how many religious the bishop anticipates will carry out the work. If, for example, the bishop needs five religious to administer a nursing home, a good phrasing for the contract would be "...at least five religious shall administer the facility, of whom one will act as administrator." This phrasing will protect the diocese in the event that one of the religious becomes ill or is removed by the major superior without a replacement.The major superior would be obliged to fulfill the provisions of the contract by assigning another religious.

The issue of just compensation for services rendered by religious is important, particularly today when many religious institutes have experienced problems in the areas of health care and retirement due to small amounts of compensation in past years. In some dioceses there are no individual stipends based on the nature of the work; religious receive a fixed stipend differing in amounts as based on a ten or twelve month apostolate. In other dioceses religious receive the same amount as the laity serving in that position. Still other dioceses have a variety of stipends depending on the type of apostolate. The National Association of Church Personnel Administrators (NACPA) located in Cincinnati, Ohio, publishes an annual list of the stipends and in kind benefits given religious across the United States. Consideration must be given to diocesan policies for housing, health and retirement benefits, transportation (e.g., car/insurance/maintenance), and other in kind benefits (e.g., a cook for the rectory or convent). It may be well to avoid putting actual figures in the contract, or at least allow for the annual increment of the stipend based on the cost of living. The financial officer of the diocese and/or the treasurers of religious institutes have expertise in this area of compensation and should be given the draft to review.

In addition to financial concerns, consideration should also be given to sick leave, vacation, retreat, and other obligations of religious life, e.g., participation in the provincial or general chapter of the institute. Having such provisions in the agreement precludes any misunderstandings, arbitrary decisions, and/or irresponsible absences on the part of the employee at unexpected times during the performance of the apostolate. It is important that the religious know to whom they report and if they have access to or the services of a secretary.

Finally, an important factor is time and termination of the contract. Sometimes there is an evaluation after the religious has been six months or less than a year in the apostolate. Such a provision affords an opportunity for the employer to give ample notice if he or she is not satisfied with the employee's performance. It also permits an opening for the religious if he or she is not satisfied or cannot adjust to the work. Likewise, it is wise to have a provision in the written contract that it be renewed annually unless the diocesan bishop or the major superior notify the other at least three or six months before the contract's renewal that the religious will be removed by one or the other from the apostolate.

If the religious is appointed to an ecclesiastical office by the diocesan bishop after presentation or assent of the major superior, the same religious can be removed by either the bishop or the major superior after advising the other authority. Canon 682 §2 reflects the dual authority exercised over the religious once he or she serves in an ecclesiastical office in a diocese. However, whether the religious has an ecclesiastical office or an apostolate in a diocese, it would seem that a contract would also include a clause indicating that either the employer (pastor or bishop) or the major superior could terminate the contract after having given due notice to the other contractant.

After the canonist draws up a draft of an agreement in accord with canon 681, it should be reviewed by the bishop and the financial officer of the diocese, the major superior and his or her council and treasurer. The canonist should consult with other appropriate persons such as pastors, administrators of apostolic works, other major superiors, and treasurers of religious institutes seeing their observations or recommendations to modify, amend, or improve the agreement prior to its final draft.

HELPFUL REFERENCES

- DePaolis, Velasio. "Schema of an Agreement for the Assignment of a Parish to Religious." *Consecrated Life* 12/1-2 (1987-1988) i:129-146; 2:218-242.

- Ghirlanda, Gianfranco, S.J. "Relations between Religious Institutes and Diocesan Bishops." *Consecrated Life* 14:1 (1989) 37-71.

- NCCB. "Proposed Guidelines on the Assessment of Clergy and Religious for Assignment." *Canon Law Newsletter* (March 1994) 3, 6-7.

Case 33

Transfer of a Religious from One Institute to Another
Canons 684-685

Case

A religious comes for an appointment to discuss the canonical procedure for a transfer. In the course of the conversation, she advises the canonist about the many difficulties she has experienced in her present institute. During summer studies, she met religious belonging to the institute she is petitioning to transfer. They seem happy, and she believes that joining them in their life and ministry will be best for her. How should the canonist advise the religious?

QUESTIONS PERTINENT TO THE CASE

1. To what institute does the religious presently belong; is it of pontifical or diocesan right?
2. Is the goal of purpose of the institute an apostolate of prayer (contemplative) or apostolic works (apostolic)?
3. Is the religious in perpetual profession; how old is she and how long has she been professed in the institute?
4. What are the difficulties she has experienced in the present institute; and has she or her major superior addressed them?
5. Why do the religious in the other institute seem happy as opposed to her?
6. What is the name of the new institute; what is its nature, spirit and purpose?
7. Has she discussed her intention with her local or major superior, a spiritual director, or a trusted friend apart from the canonist?
8. Has she spoken to the superior in the institute to which she plans to transfer?
9. What is the condition of her health; has she visited medical doctors or sought the assistance of a counselor in this period of crisis or transition?
10. Has she considered some of the practical difficulties attendant on transfer?

THE LAW

Can. 684 §1. A member in perpetual vows cannot transfer from one

165

religious institute to another except by a grant of the supreme moderator of each institute and with the consent of their respective councils.

§2. After completing a probation which is to last at least three years, the member can be admitted to perpetual profession in the new institute. If the member refuses to make this profession or is not admitted to make it by competent superiors, however, the member is to return to the original institute unless an indult of secularization has been obtained.

§3. For a religious to transfer from an autonomous monastery to another of the same institute or federation or confederation, the consent of the major superior of each monastery and of the chapter of the receiving monastery is required and is sufficient, without prejudice to other requirements established by proper law; a new profession is not required.

§4. Proper law is to determine the time and manner of the probation which must precede the profession of a member in the new institute.

§5. For a transfer to be made to a secular institute or a society of apostolic life or from them to a religious institute, permission of the Holy See is required, whose mandates must be observed.

Can. 685 §1. Until a person makes profession in the new institute, the rights and obligations which the member had in the former institute are suspended although the vows remain. Nevertheless, from the beginning of probation, the member is bound to the observance of the proper law of the new institute.

§2. Through profession in the new institute, the member is incorporated into it while the preceding vows, rights, and obligations cease.

COMMENTARY

It would be important to consider first what transfer involves. While the religious believes she remains called to live religious life, she believes the Spirit is directing her to another juridical structure different from the one to which she committed herself to initially. Perhaps the key question of the canonist would be: "What attracts you to the spirituality or charism of that institute?" If the religious is transferring simply to move away from the difficulties she is presently experiencing, she must understand she brings herself to the new institute in which she will be obliged to live common life and observe the evangelical counsels in accord with its proper law. If her problems stem from living the communal life or are resultant from the obligations of one or more of the evangelical counsels, it may be important for her to examine her vocation to religious life.

Another consideration here is the permission of the general superiors to transfer. If the sister has consistently experienced difficulties in religious life, then it would seem that the major superior and councilors of the institute in which she is professed could not with integrity permit her to transfer to the other institute. Or, if they give permission reluctantly, honesty would direct them to convey to the major superior of the new institute the difficulties the sister experiences in her religious life. If this be the case, it would seem the general superior of the new institute may decide not to permit the transfer. The sister's difficulties should be addressed in the institute to which she belongs, or she could petition for exclaustration if she needs objectivity to address these issues. Simply to move from one religious institute to another does not resolve difficulties with religious life, and such problems will only surface later as the religious settles into the new institute.

A serious concern, even with successful transfers is what this canonist refers to as "memory lane." Religious who transfer successfully, because of a strong attraction to another way of living religious life or because the initial institute failed to renew and adapt in accord with conciliar and post conciliar teachings of the Church, have admitted that their main difficulty was in the failure to identify with the past memorable events of those religious who entered at the prescribed times and passed through candidacy, novitiate, and temporary profession in the institute. The religious who transferred had no frame of reference for these past experiences that were recalled at jubilees and other social events in the institute. This issue should be brought to the attention of any religious thinking of transferring so that he or she will not begin the process without recognizing the inevitable effects of the significant change effected in a transfer.

Since the transfer is between two religious institutes and not to another form of consecrated life (c. 684 §5), the general superiors grant the transfer having obtained the consent of their respective councils. The other canonical provisions in the two norms above must be followed: the member must be in perpetual profession (unless it is a transfer from a monastery of the same institute, federation, or confederation), she must complete a probationary period lasting at least three years according to the proper law of the new institute, and she is admitted to perpetual profession by the competent superior in the new institute (c. 684 §1, §2. §3). If during the probationary period the religious is not satisfied, or if the competent superior of the new institute judges her unsuitable for the life of the new institute, the sister must return to her own institute or seek an indult of departure (c. 684 §1), since she is still legally bound to the former institute.

During the probationary period, the religious is obliged to the observances described in the proper law of the new institute (c. 685 §1); the rights and obligations she enjoyed in the former institute are suspended during this time of probation. If she is satisfied living the life in the new institute and is judged suitable by the competent authorities, she will be admitted to perpetual profession with the completion of the probationary period. At that time the rights and obligations of the former institute cease, while she assumes the rights and obligations in the new institute through profession (c. 654).

At this juncture, it is important that the major superior of the new institute contact the major superior of the former institute, advising her of the perpetual profession of the member. Personal papers such as acts of cession, will, act of renunciation (if the nature of the institute required this), living will, durable power of attorney would be sent to the religious in order that she revise them in accord with the provisions of the new institute. Likewise, if the sister has any patrimony, this should be transferred to the new institute. If the sister is admitted to solemn vows, i.e. she is required to make a renunciation of her patrimony, disposing of it as she sees fit prior to her solemn perpetual profession (c. 668 §4).

HELPFUL REFERENCES

- Abbass, John, OFM, Conv. "Transfer to another religious institute in the latin and eastern catholic churches." *Commentarium pro Religiosis et Missionariis* 79/1 (1998) 121-151.

- Hill, Richard A. "Transfers of Religious." *Review for Religious* 44 (1985) 929-932.

- McDermott, Rose. "The Role of Major Superiors in the Transfer of Religious and the Admission of Former Members." *Bulletin on Issues of Religious Law* 15 (Fall 1998) 1-4.

- _____ . "Transfer-Canons 684-685." *Bulletin on Issues of Religious Law* 5/1 (April 1989) 1-7.

- Smith, Rosemary, S.C. "Separation and Transfer of Religious: Context and Procedure." *CLSA Proceedings of the Forty-seventh Annual Convention* (October 15-18, 1985) 97-114.

TRANSFER - PERMISSION OF SUPERIOR GENERAL

I, Sister _____, general superior of the _____ Congregation, having consulted the provincial superior _____, and obtained the consent of the council in accord with canon 684 §1 grant Sister _____ of perpetual profession in our congregation permission to transfer to the _____ Monastery in order to begin a probationary period prior to perpetual profession.

During her twenty-five years in our institute, sister has been a faithful religious in the obligations of communal and vowed life according to our *Constitutions*. Sister's departure is a grave loss for us, be we respect her decision to begin the contemplative life of a cloistered religious.

If sister perseveres and is professed in the same monastery after the prescribed probationary period, I ask that our congregation be informed of the date of her profession in order to complete our file and to send the appropriate papers to the said Monastery.

_____

General Superior

TRANSFER - ACCEPTANCE OF MAJOR SUPERIOR OF MONASTERY

I, Sister _____, major superior of the Monastery of _____, having procured the consent of the council and our chapter in accord with canon 684 §1, give Sister _____ permission to enter our monastery and begin her probationary period as a cloistered contemplative nun.

According to our *Constitutions*, Sister _____ will have a four year probationary period. If she perseveres and is judged suitable for our life, she shall be admitted to solemn perpetual profession. Prior to her profession, sister will be obliged to make an act of renunciation in accord with our *Constitutions*. We will notify the general superior of sister's former institute regarding her solemn perpetual profession and request any documents in her file that need adjustment to religious life in the monastery.

_____
Major Superior

Case 34

Extension of Exclaustration
Canon 686 §1

Case

A sister calls and asks for an appointment with a canonist. She has been on exclaustration for three years and would like her superior general to afford her more time. She explains that the had been depressed in the institute and the major superior advised her to see a therapist During the counseling sessions, it became apparent that the depression stemmed from abuse in her early childhood. She needs more time to address this revelation, but believes the major superior would not be open to the extension of the exclaustration.

QUESTIONS PERTINENT TO THE CASE

1. What is the name of the institute; is it of pontifical or diocesan right?
2. Why did she petition exclaustration; could the depression have been addressed by the psychologist/psychiatrist while she remained living in the institute?
3. What has she been doing these past three years apart from the institute?
4. Has she been depressed during these three years, and would she think that community life may be more supportive than living alone?
5. Has she been able to support herself; how is the cost of the therapist being handled?
6. Has the religious ever shared the discovery of abuse in childhood with the major superior of her institute?
7. Is the general superior in this country, or is she depending on consultation with the provincial superior; did sister report to the latter the abuse discovered during counseling?
8. Does she have any family members or are the members of the institute her sole support during this difficult period?
9. Does she feel welcome to return periodically to a house of the institute; is she invited to return for spiritual or social events?
10. How old is sister, and what is the condition of her physical health at this time?

171

11. Has she the assistance of a spiritual director or a good friend at this difficult time?

THE LAW

Can. 670 An institute must supply the members with all those things which are necessary to achieve the purpose of their vocation, according to the norm of the constitutions.

Can. 686 §1. With the consent of the council, the supreme moderator for a grave cause can grant an indult of exclaustration to a member professed by perpetual vows, but not for more than three years, and if it concerns a cleric, with the prior consent of the ordinary of the place in which he must reside. To extend an indult or to grant it for more than three years is reserved to the Holy See, or to the diocesan bishop if it concerns institutes of diocesan right.

§2. It is only for the Apostolic See to grant an indult of exclaustration for nuns.

COMMENTARY

The questions above would assist the canonist in obtaining a sense of how the religious has spent her years on exclaustration and if they were beneficial to her in this difficulty. Likewise, the conversation should give some insight into her openness with the major superiors of the institute, their provision and kindness to her, and a sense of whether it may be good for her to live apart or to live within a supportive community at this time. Certainly there seems to be grave cause, if additional time of exclaustration seems feasible, to grant the indult beyond the three years given by the general superior. However, it is reasonable to ask if the sister could return to the institute and continue her therapy within the security of communal life. It would seem that at this difficult time she needs the support and understanding of kind persons as she goes through the challenging time of counseling and healing.

On the other hand, some persons going through such a demanding process need solitude and privacy in which to sort out their lives; the demands of community life and apostolic service may preclude or inhibit such quiet space apart. The uncovering of sexual abuse in childhood often brings all of life's decisions into sharp focus, including one's vocation. This woman certainly needs the spiritual, emotional, and perhaps financial support of her religious family during this time. If she has been in the religious institute for a significant number of years, the institute is her family, but she must be open with the major superior in order to gain this support.

If exclaustration would be the more feasible solution for the sister, it would seem unjust not to support her petition. The major superior (provincial superior) should send her and the council's opinion for or against the extension to the general superior. This greatly helps the general superior and her council in sending their opinion to CICLSAL or to the diocesan bishop. If the major superior (provincial superior) and council are not supportive of the sister's request, the member could take recourse to the general superior of the institute, having informed the provincial superior of her intent to do so. Likewise, if the superior general and council do not support the extension of exclaustration, the religious has the right of recourse to CICLSAL or the diocesan bishop depending on the canonical status of the institute (pontifical or diocesan right).

The provincial superior should have the religious write a petition, sending it with the opinion of the provincial and council to the general superior. If the only major superior is the general superior, she would send the petition of the religious with the her opinion and that of her council to CICLSAL or to the diocesan bishop (c. 686 §3).

Above all, it is important that the religious be open and honest with the major superiors in this matter. She should be advised that they are bound to protect her privacy (c. 220), and that her conversations with them are confidential. If she is not open, the major superior may think that she is simply procrastinating in not returning to the institute or seeking definitive departure from it. Sister needs the spiritual, emotional, and perhaps financial support of the institute at this troublesome time.

HELPFUL REFERENCES

• See articles on exclaustration on p. 68.

SAMPLE

REQUEST FOR EXTENSION OF EXCLAUSTRATION

I, Sister _____, a perpetually professed religious in the congregation of _____, pontifical right in the diocese of _____, petition for an extension of my indult of exclaustration granted by my superior general for a period of three years from _____ to _____, for the same reason.

During the past six years of my religious life, I have been unable to live quality life in community due to severe depression. Counseling sessions with an experienced therapist have led me to recognize that the depression stems from abuse I received as a child. This has been a traumatic revelation for me, and I need time to address this tragedy and heal apart from the demands of community life and apostolic activity. My major superiors have been most supportive of me during this challenging period. Likewise, I have sought the advice of a canonist and a spiritual director; both have been most helpful to me. I plan to spend this time in the most productive manner to regain my self-esteem and emotional health.

Thank you, Cardinal _____ for the consideration you give my request and for your ongoing assistance to religious.

_____   _____

Date   Signature

SAMPLE

SUPPORTING STATEMENT OF THE SUPERIOR GENERAL

I, Sister _____, General Superior of the Sisters of _____ recommend the enclosed petition for our Sister _____. Sister has been an exemplary member of our institute until the last six years when she gave evidence of severe depression. While we thought it best for her to receive counseling within the supportive confines of our institute, the demands of communal life and an apostolate took their toll on sister. During the past three years, she has kept in touch with me and is most accountable regarding her life apart from the institute. She seems to have handled her situation well, and is receiving very fine professional guidance. I have consulted sister's therapist regarding the best environment for sister to regain her emotional health, and he assures me that this time away will be productive for her.

The councilors and I firmly believe that, whatever sister's final decision will be, we are her family and support at this time. Likewise, we want to offer her any spiritual, emotional, or financial support she may need to surmount this crisis in her life. Having discussed the matter with my council, they join me in recommending that an extension of the indult of exclaustration be given sister to continue to address this tragic discovery in her life.

_____   _____
Date   Signature

175

Case 35

Extension of Exclaustration Denied
Canon 686 §1

Case

A provincial superior calls a canonist to advise that two of the institute's members on exclaustration have been living together for the past three years. While they were in the institute, gossip arose in the local community regarding their relationship, prompting each of them to seek exclaustration. Since the three years of exclaustration are coming to a close, they are petitioning to return and live together in the institute; otherwise, they will ask for an extension of exclaustration. The major superior asks the canonist's advice.

QUESTIONS PERTINENT TO THE CASE

1. Is the institute of pontifical or diocesan right?
2. Are the religious clerics or lay members?
3. How old are the religious and how long have they been in perpetual profession?
4. What was the nature of the "gossip" that arose in the local community prior to their departure?
5. Was the situation addressed before they were granted exclaustration; was any counseling offered to either of the religious?
6. Does the major superior believe the "gossip" prompted the religious' petitions for exclaustration?
7. Have they been in touch with the provincial superior; has the provincial superior attempted to meet with each of them separately?
8. Have they kept in touch with the major superior or a delegated religious during their time of exclaustration?
9. How did the provincial superior learn of their proposal?
10. Is the general superior of the institute aware of this situation?

THE LAW

> Can. 686 §1. With the consent of the council, the supreme moderator for a grave cause can grant an indult of exclaustration to a member professed by perpetual vows, but not for more than three years, and if it concerns a cleric,

177

with the prior consent of the ordinary of the place in which he must reside. To extend an indult or to grant it for more than three years is reserved to the Holy See, or to the diocesan bishop if it concerns institutes of diocesan right.

COMMENTARY

It would seem from the request of the two religious that they do not want to be separated whether within or beyond the religious institute. One of the important factors here would be for the provincial superior to address each of these religious separately to be certain that the religious is making a free decision unimpaired by pressure from the other. Each of these religious must recognize that the decision he or she makes has serious implications for the remainder of his or her life.

The canonist should advise the major superior, if it is the provincial level of the institute, that an extension of exclaustration for the reason offered by the two religious should not be recommended to the general superior. The time of exclaustration is given for a religious to make a prudential judgement concerning his or her continuance in religious life or definitive departure. The canonical institution of exclaustration should not be compromised by recommending it be given for two religious who have already decided that they want religious life on their own terms. These religious are not in a discernment process regarding their religious vocations; they have already decided the way they wish to continue living whether in or beyond the institute. Their decision has grave implications for the obligations of common life and the public vows of religious life.

The canonist should also advise the major superior that there is no possibility of these religious returning to the institute with a condition attached, i.e., to live together in a local community within the institute. When a person decides that he or she is called to religious life, there must be a total gift or self-donation to Christ in service to his people. This total gift of self cannot be made with conditions attached; there is absolute trust in Divine Providence on the part of the religious. Therefore, it would be impossible and irresponsible for any major superior to consider permitting religious to return to the communal life of the institute under such a condition. Not only would such a condition be contrary to the vows and the obligation of common life, it would impede a superior from the obligation and right to mission one or both of these religious.

Perhaps the provincial superior should visit the religious or request that they come to the provincial site for an appointment. After meeting with each individually, the major superior should make it clear that the two options they presented are most unsuitable and incongruent with religious life. Exclaustration is a time of discernment - to decide to return to religious life or to seek definitive departure. These religious have already decided that they wish to spend their lives together, and it is not possible to return to the religious institute with the conditions attached. Each has to decide on her own whether to seek an indult of departure from the religious institute or to return with no conditions attached to live the life and perform the apostolate of the institute.

The opinion of the superior general and council accompanying the indults of departure sent to CICLSAL should include these facts. It should advise that counseling was offered but rejected by the religious, that they were interviewed separately, and that they had three years of exclaustration in which to come to a decision regarding their vocations. Since they seem adamant in living together either in religious life or apart from it, the indult of departure would be in the best interests of the religious and the institute. The equity and charity of the gospel should be accorded these sisters in keeping with the policy of the institute regarding canon 702 §2.

HELPFUL REFERENCES

- McDermott, Rose. "Dealing with Difficult Religious." *Bulletin on Issues of Religious Law* (October 1987) 1-9.

- McDonough, Elizabeth. "Voluntary Exclaustration." *Review for Religious* 51/3 (May-June 1992) 461-469.

- Torres, Jesus. "Procedure for the Exclaustration of a Religious." *Consecrated Life* 18/1 (1993) 47-73.

Case 36

Imposed Exclaustration of a
Member of an Institute of Diocesan Right
Canon 686 §3

Case

A member forty years professed in a religious institute of diocesan right has been living apart from the communal life of the institute and working in hospital ministry as a psychiatric nurse. Little by little her relationship with her religious institute began to deteriorate. She did not attend meetings, refused to propose a budget for her expenses, and eventually kept the entire salary paid for her service in the health care facility. Requests from the general treasurer and visits by the major superior met with little or no results. When the major superior met with the council, they understood that sister could be dismissed from the institute in accord with canon 696 §1 for grave failures in obedience and poverty. Mindful of her years in religious life and apostolic service, and the fact that she is in her early sixties, they decided to request imposed exclaustration. They believed that this condition of life would more appropriately reflect sister's lifestyle.

QUESTIONS PERTINENT TO THE CASE

1. In what diocese is the generalate of the institute located?
2. What has been the general pattern of sister in the institute during her thirty-five years?
3. Did sister receive permission to live apart from the institute, or did she initiate this on her own?
4. How long has sister been living apart from the institute; have any efforts been made to have her return to communal living?
5. How old was sister when she entered; did she receive her professional training in the institute?
6. Has sister received any counseling in the past; is she under pressure as a psychiatric nurse in the hospital?
7. What is the state of her health?
8. What kind of lifestyle does she live; is she extravagant or does she live frugally?

9. Has the sister ever given reasons for her aloofness from the institute?
10. Has sister any friends apart from the members of her institute; does she meet or socialize with any sisters in the institute?

> Can. 686 §3. At the petition of the supreme moderator with the consent of the council, exclaustration can be imposed by the Holy See on a member of an institute of pontifical right, or by a diocesan bishop on a member of an institute of diocesan right, for grave causes, with equity and charity observed.

> Can. 687 An exclaustrated member is considered freed from the obligations which cannot be reconciled with the new condition of his or her life, yet remains dependent upon and under the care of superiors and also of the local ordinary, especially if the member is a cleric. The member can wear the habit of the institute unless the indult determines otherwise. Nevertheless, the member lacks active and passive voice.

COMMENTARY

It would be well first to hear the responses to some of the above questions in order to obtain a better understanding of the case. Has sister been a faithful religious up until the time of this assignment? Did she insist on living apart from the institute or was she given permission to do so in accord with canon 665 §1 of the code? Did communications break down because initially those responsible did not keep in contact with the sister? How is she living, and what would be her need for her entire salary; does she realize this is contrary to her vow of poverty (c. 668 §3)? Does the major superior or any member of the council think that she may be under severe stress due to the nature of her work? How long has she been serving in the capacity of a psychiatric nurse? What is the condition of her general health?

The superior general should meet with the council and discuss all of the above. If the sister is truly culpable and all efforts to contact her or encourage her to budget and turn her salary over to the institute fail, she could well be liable for dismissal from the institute. However, her health, both physical and psychological, must be studied. It may help to have a member of the institute close to the sister attempt to talk with her. If all fails, the superior general and council may consider that she has lived as a religious for forty years and that she is close to sixty years of age. For these reasons, they may decide on the more benevolent decision that would reflect her present way of living, i.e., enforced exclaustration.

If asked to be an advocate in such cases, this canonist should carefully explain that the sister's failure to cooperate with her major superior regarding the obligations of religious life are grave reasons that could prompt the same superior to begin a dismissal process. The canonist could recommend that the religious consider petitioning for an indult of exclaustration from the general superior for a three year period in order to evaluate her vocation to the religious institute (c. 686 §1). If the sister refuses this suggestion, the general superior with the consent of the council can petition the diocesan bishop for imposed exclaustration. In the petition, the superior should explain the grave reasons for the request, the years of service of the religious, and the general council's reluctance to initiate a dismissal process, and their willingness to accept a periodic evaluation of the sister's experience on exclaustration. It would seem, that given the salary she receives as a psychiatric nurse, she would be able to care for her needs as a religious on exclaustration.

If the sister cannot be exhorted to regularize her way of life either by cooperating with the general council and returning to her religious institute or by petitioning for an indult of exclaustration, the superior general and council should meet and decide what to do. Admittedly, there are grounds for dismissal in accord with canon 696 §1, i.e., "habitual neglect of the obligations of consecrated life, repeated violations of the sacred bonds, stubborn disobedience to the legitimate prescripts of superiors in a grave matter." However, there are times when a superior general in discussion with the council may lean toward equity and charity based on the age of the religious and her notable years in the institute. In such instances, a more charitable route would be to petition ecclesiastical authority for an indefinite period of exclaustration.

If the religious does not cooperate, and a decision is reached to petition for enforced or imposed exclaustration (c. 686 §3), the superior general must have the consent of an absolute majority of the councilors in order to petition the imposition of exclaustration from the diocesan bishop. This means that if there are four councilors, three must vote in the affirmative (c. 127 §1) in order for the superior general to act. It would be well, too, for the general council to understand that in voting for imposed exclaustration, the institute remains responsible for the welfare of the sister. While the religious remains free from obligations that cannot be reconciled with this new condition (e.g., community life in common, turning over one's earnings), the religious remains under the care of the major superior. The sister lacks active and passive voice, since she is not living the common life of the institute (c. 687). Sister retains her own salary, she must pay taxes and is responsible for herself regarding health care, car insurance, etc. It is important that this distancing be maintained in order to protect the institute against liability. It should be understood that if she cannot manage for herself in illness or advanced age, she can return to the institute. The major superior should communicate with the diocesan bishop of the place in which the sister resides advising him that she is on exclaustration, under his pastoral care and the care of her major superior (c. 687).

- Sharon Holland, IHM. "Chapter VI Separation of Members from the Institute (cc. 684-704)." *New Commentary on the Code of Canon Law* edited by John P. Beal, James A. Coriden, and Thomas J. Green. New York/Mahwah: Paulist Press, 2000:856-858.

SAMPLE

LETTER OF THE SUPERIOR GENERAL

Dear Bishop _____,

I deeply regret that, having obtained the consent of my council on _____, I request that exclaustration be imposed on Sister _____, a perpetually professed member of our religious congregation in accord with canon 686 §3 of the Code of Canon Law for the following reasons.

Sister has been a member of our congregation for forty years and is sixty years old. She is presently ministering as a psychiatric nurse in _____, a health care facility in the diocese of _____. Gradually sister has disengaged herself from the life of our institute, refusing to attend meetings, to respond to reasonable requests, to return to communal living within close range of the hospital, and to send in her salary and petition a budget for her expenditures. All of these refusals are contrary to the proper law and the policies of our religious institute. Moreover, some are grave failures against the vows sister professed at the beginning of her religious life. All attempts on our part and the part of the former administration have met with failure on sister's part to communicate or cooperate. When I recently asked sister to consider petitioning for voluntary exclaustration to reflect the lifestyle she is living, she refused.

The councilors and I discussed the above at length and recognize that such behavior on the part of sister could well merit dismissal from our congregation. However, given her age and her many years of service in health care as a member of our congregation, we hesitate to take this drastic measure. Instead, we ask that, since sister did not petition for voluntary exclaustration, exclaustration be imposed on her in accord with canon 686 §3 of the Code of Canon Law. In petitioning for this, we recognize that sister remains a member and under the care of the major superior of this congregation. In her advanced age or illness, she is free to return to our congregation for care. Since sister has kept her substantial salary for the past four years, it would seem that she does not at present require financial assistance from us.

We thank you, Bishop _____, for considering this regrettable request, and we ask that you continue to keep sister and all of our members in your prayer.

SAMPLE

DECREE OF IMPOSED EXCLAUSTRATION

Sister _____, a member in perpetual profession of the Congregation of _____ has been requested by her superior general to consider petitioning for exclaustration in order that her canonical status be in keeping with her present way of living. Sister has remained aloof from her institute, refuses to communicate or visit, retains her salary, and refuses to return to a house of the institute near her place of work. Since sister refused to petition for voluntary exclaustration, Sister _____, the general superior of the congregation having secured the unanimous consent of her council requested of me in a letter dated _____ that exclaustration be imposed on Sister _____ for the reasons above.

Having studied the matter carefully, exclaustration is imposed on Sister _____ in accord with canon 686 §3 of the Code of Canon Law. This imposed exclaustration is given for the sake of common life and that equity and charity be accorded to all concerned. Moreover, exclaustration more fittingly becomes the lifestyle that sister has chosen to live which is contrary to the common life required of religious in canon 665 of the Code of Canon Law. The effects of this imposed exclaustration are described in canon 687, i.e., sister is freed from those obligations irreconcilable with her condition of life and lacks active and passive voice in the institute. Nevertheless, she remains dependent upon and under the care of her superiors and the diocesan bishop of the place wherein she resides. This exclaustration will remain in effect until illness or advanced age would necessitate her return to common life.

Given on _____ day of _____ month in the year _____ .

_____
Bishop of _____

Case 37

Exclusion from Subsequent Profession
Canon 689

Case

A provincial superior calls to ask the advice of a canonist regarding a religious in temporary profession. He is most disruptive of the common life of the local house, and the provincial superior would like to begin a dismissal process. The religious made temporary profession for three years and has completed a year and a half. What advice should the canonist offer?

QUESTIONS PERTINENT TO THE CASE

1. Is this a clerical or lay institute; is it of diocesan or pontifical right?
2. How long has the member been in the institute besides the year and a half of temporary profession?
3. What is the status of the religious; did he enter as a cleric?
4. What does the provincial superior mean by "disruptive" behavior?
5. Has the religious been warned of his behavior; has he been offered any counseling to address it?
6. What has been the evaluation of this religious prior to his entrance, by the formation personnel, and religious superiors during his entire probationary period?
7. Have the evaluations of these competent persons been shared with the religious?
8. What are the procedures in the province for those advancing through the formation period?
9. Is there a norm in the proper law of the religious institute that addresses the dismissal of a member in temporary profession (c. 696 §2)?
10. Who has the authority to admit or exclude from subsequent profession in the institute; is that superior required to obtain the advice or consent of the counsel?
11. If the general superior admits or excludes a member from subsequent profession; what is the role of the provincial superior?
12. How long is the time of temporary profession in the institute?

Can. 689 §1. If there are just causes, the competent major superior, after having heard the council, can exclude a member from making a subsequent profession when the period of temporary profession has been completed.

§2. Physical or psychic illness, even contracted after profession, which in the judgment of experts renders the member mentioned in §1 unsuited to lead the life of the institute constitutes a cause for not admitting the member to renew profession or to make perpetual profession, unless the illness had been contracted through the negligence of the institute or through work performed in the institute. §3. If, however, a religious becomes insane during the period of temporary vows, even though unable to make a new profession, the religious cannot be dismissed from the institute.

COMMENTARY

It would be important first to learn the canonical status of the institute and to request both the proper law of the institute and whatever directory or policy the institute has on formation and the process for a candidate to advance from one formative stage to another. Likewise, one must know the background of the member since his entrance to the institute. A dismissal process is always demanding and draining on all concerned. It should rarely be advised for one in temporary profession, since it seems to raise questions as to why the member was admitted to the institute in the first place. Even in the case of those in perpetual profession, if dismissal seems obvious due to grave imputable offenses, a canonist would suggest that since the person does not want to live the religious life in accord with canon and proper laws, it is best to petition for an indult of departure and avoid the stigma of dismissal from the institute. However, voluntary departure cannot be forced either on those in temporary or those in perpetual profession, as it would be an invalid departure.

If the institute has a good procedure in place for admitting persons to first and subsequent profession, the religious should have been informed by competent authorities and formation personnel that his reprehensible behavior does not measure up to the standards of the institute. Likewise, he should have been offered some help to address the behavioral patterns, and there should be available follow-up reports on his progress. He should be made aware every step of the way that his conduct is unsuitable for the communal life of the institute.

If help has been offered the individual and the competent formation personnel and major superior have followed the procedures for advancing him through the stages of formation without success, it would seem that this person is not suited for the life of the institute. The proper law of the institute would determine the length of time required in temporary profession before admission to final or perpetual profession (c. 655). However, the complex procedure of facultative dismissal (c. 696) should not be recommended.

Instead, the provincial superior with the provincial vicar or first assistant should meet with the religious in temporary profession. The superior should once again put before the religious the reports of the difficulties the members of the institute are experiencing with his conduct, giving him examples of the same. The superior should advise the religious that the institute has tried in vain to assist him in correcting this behavior. This may be because the member has refused the counseling or has failed to integrate the help derived from it in his manner of acting. The provincial superior should advise him that he is not welcome in the institute, and he will not be recommended (if the general superior admits) or admitted (if the provincial superior admits) to subsequent profession when the time of his temporary profession is completed (c. 689 §1).

The major superior should advise the religious that he will not be dismissed, but it is fruitless for him to waste time remaining in the institute. The province will assist him with counseling and returning to life outside the institute. The religious must voluntarily request departure from the institute (c. 688 §2) and a could be given permission to depart the common life of the institute until the vows expire (c. 665 §1). Parameters should be placed on financial assistance depending on the time spent in the institute, the counseling already given the member, institute's policies, and the education, etc. he received in the institute. The religious should be permitted to make plans for a smooth withdrawal from the institute in seeking employment, procuring residence, and planning for his future lifestyle. In choosing to remain in the institute, the member only wastes time and avoids the opportunity to make plans for the future. If he chooses to remain until the vows expire, he must be advised by the major superior that during that time he must conduct himself in accord with what is expected of a member of the institute.

When a religious in temporary profession realizes that there is no hope for subsequent profession in the institute and he or she is simply wasting time, the religious is willing to cooperate with the assistance given and begins to plan for life outside the institute. Frequently a religious in such a situation comes to realize that the best opportunities in his or her life for growth in human maturity were experienced through the lived example and assistance offered by the religious institute.

A case like this is salutary for both major superiors and formation personnel. It calls for their vigilance in admitting candidates to the institute (c. 642). It is important to remember that even those in first profession are members of an institute with certain rights as well as obligations (cc. 654, 688). Vowed religious cannot be dismissed without complex canonical procedures. However, temporary professed members can be excluded from making subsequent profession as canon 689 §1 provides. Often the problem lies in admitting to temporary profession for a period of three years rather than one year at a time. If a problem begins the first year of profession, and the religious made profession for only one year, he or she can be refused the renewal or further profession in the institute. If the religious made profession for three years, he or she cannot be dismissed until the expiration of the three years except through the canonical process. However, if the religious is addressed in a way that reflects concern and kindness for his or her well-being as a member of the Christian faithful, it would seem that the member will come to understand that his or her behavioral pattern in communal living is totally incongruent with religious life.

HELPFUL REFERENCES

- CICLSAL. Directive, *Potissimum institutioni,* February 2, 1990: *AAS* 82 (1990) 470-532. English translation in *Origins* 19 (1990) 677, 679-699.

- Hill, Richard. "Denial of Profession." *Review for Religious* 47 (1988) 934-938.

- _____ . "Screening the Candidates: The Need to Know." *Review for Religious* 45 (1986) 458-462.

- Loftus, J. A. "Victims of Abuse as Candidates." *Review for Religious* 45 (1986) 725-738.

- McDermott, Rose. "Dealing with the Difficult Religious." *Bulletin on Issues of Religious Law* (October 1987) 1-9.

Case 38

Readmission to a Religious Institute
Canon 690

Case

A woman in her late fifties requests to be readmitted to a religious congregation that she departed over twenty years ago. During those years she has taught in a public school and earned a pension from the public school retirement fund. What would be some issues that the vocation director should keep in mind as she proceeds to interview the woman?

QUESTIONS PERTINENT TO THE CASE

1. How long had the woman been in the religious congregation prior to departure?
2. Did she legitimately depart the institute; was she dismissed?
3. What does her file indicate regarding the quality of life she led while in the institute; were there any outstanding difficulties with others, with ministry?
4. What was the reason for her departure; has she resolved any difficulty that may have led to her departure; how long has she been considering readmittance?
5. Apart from teaching in public school, what has been the quality of her life during these past ten years?
6. Did she marry or enter any other institute of consecrated life?
7. Is she registered in a parish, active in the parish? Would her pastor know her and support her readmittance?
8. Does she have a spiritual director?
9. Has she kept in close contact with friends she made while in the institute?
10. Is she an associate of the institute?
11. Does she recognize that during the twenty years she remained apart from the institute it has grown and developed?
12. What is the woman's state of health at this time; does she have any family members dependent on her?

Can. 690 §1. The supreme moderator with the consent of the council can readmit without the burden of repeating the novitiate one who had legitimately left the institute after completing the novitiate or after profession. Moreover, it will be for the same moderator to determine an appropriate probation prior to temporary profession and the time of vows to precede perpetual profession, according to the norm of cann. 655 and 657.

§2. The superior of an autonomous monastery with the consent of the council possesses the same faculty.

COMMENTARY

First it would be important to have a sense of the woman's experience in the religious congregation. How long had she lived in the institute, and at what stage did she depart: postulancy, novitiate, temporary profession, or perpetual profession? The reason she left would be extremely important - did she depart voluntarily or was she dismissed? Was she sent away as a postulant or novice? The vocation director would do well to check the files to obtain information regarding the woman before meeting with her. If there were problems while the woman lived in the institute, it would be important to see if they have been resolved in the past years.

The vocation director should gain a sense of how the woman has spent the last twenty years. Apart from teaching, what has occurred in her life? Did she marry or was she admitted to another institute of consecrated life, as it could well be that an invalidating impediment exists barring her readmission. Has she practiced her faith; is she active in her parish; does she volunteer her services for any parish or diocesan events? Has she maintained friendships with some of the members of the institute during her separation from it? Are there any family members that depend on her emotional and monetary support?

After the vocation director collects information regarding the woman's life in and beyond the institute, it would be well to explain to her that during the past twenty years the institute has evolved. The woman cannot expect to find the institute at exactly the same place it was twenty years ago; she will find some notable differences and must understand this. It may be well also to remind her that she, too, has developed as a person. Over the past twenty years, she has been living a life of relative independence; it may be a difficult adjustment for her at this age to embrace the obligations of the evangelical counsels.

Finally, the director should explain the procedure involved if the major superior decides to readmit the woman. If she completed the novitiate before she departed, she would not have to repeat the novitiate. However, there would be a probationary period and then a period of time in temporary profession in accord with canons 655 and 657. Here some canonists refer to *Renovationis causam* 38 (2), and conclude that the time required in temporary profession would be no less than a year or no less than the period of temporary probation which she would have had to complete before profession at the time of the institute. However, this canonist is of the opinion that the time spent in temporary profession would be in accord with the present law, i.e., at least three years, unless the major superior decides to seek a dispensation from that norm for the woman. Following her time spent in temporary profession, if she is suitable and willing, she would be admitted to perpetual profession in the institute.

If all goes well and the woman is readmitted, it is well to advise her not to dispose of her temporal goods until she sees if she is willing to persevere in religious life and the institute is willing to receive her as member in perpetual profession. At times, men or women at entrance divest themselves of all their temporalities and have nothing if they are dissatisfied with religious life or if they are asked to leave the institute. If judged suitable and admitted to first profession, she would make an act of cession and cede the administration of her goods to whomever she prefers in accord with the norms of proper law; prior to perpetual profession, she would make a will valid in civil law (c. 668 §1). The pension she earned as a teacher beyond the institute remains part of her patrimony; if she so decides, it can be directed to the retirement fund of the institute (c. 668 §1).

HELPFUL REFERENCES

- Hill, Richard A. "Admitting Former Members." *Review for Religious* 45 (1986) 621-524.

- McDermott, Rose. "The Role of Major Superiors in the Transfer of Religious and the Admission of Former Members." *Bulletin on Issues of Religious Law* 15 (Fall 1998) 1-6.

Case 39

Indult of Departure of a Clerical Religious
without a Benevolent Bishop
Canon 691

Case

A provincial superior of a clerical religious institute advises a canonist that one of the members petitioned and received a leave of absence some twelve years ago, but never returned. When he is finally contacted, the religious informs the provincial superior that he is successful in a small business and does not want to return to the religious institute. However, he does not want to go through the process of laicization, since someone advised him it is a long, gruelling process. The major superior asks the canonist how he can regularize the status of this member.

QUESTIONS PERTINENT TO THE CASE

1. Was the member ordained and incardinated in the clerical religious institute; is the institute of pontifical right?
2. Is the member in perpetual vows; was he ordained to the priesthood in the institute?
3. What was the initial reason for the permission to live apart from the common life of the religious institute?
4. Were any parameters of time or condition placed on the permission to leave?
5. Did any of the major superiors attempt to contact him over the twelve year period; has he had any contact with members of the religious institute?
6. Did the cleric refuse to return when asked; were there any follow-ups to the refusal?
7. Can the provincial superior give an account of the behavioral pattern of the member during the time he spent in the institute?
8. Has the member married, or does he have the intention of marrying at some time?
9. Does he live with anyone or have an intimate relationship with any person?
10. If contented with his present life, would he be willing to petition for an indult

of departure from the Apostolic See?

THE LAW

Can. 691 §1. A perpetually professed religious is not to request an indult of departure from an institute except for the gravest of causes considered before the Lord. The religious is to present a petition to the supreme moderator of the institute who is to transmit it along with a personal opinion and the opinion of the council to the competent authority.

§2. In institutes of pontifical right, an indult of this type is reserved to the Apostolic See. In institutes of diocesan right, however, the bishop of the diocese in which the house of assignment is situated can also grant it.

Can. 692 Unless it has been rejected by the member in the act of notification, an indult of departure granted legitimately and made known to the member entails by the law itself dispensation from the vows and from all the obligations arising from profession.

COMMENTARY

In speaking with the provincial superior it would be important first to know the canonical status of the institute and that of the member, as well as a brief account of the member's behavior while living the common life of the institute. It would be important to know the length of time spent in the institute, the man's age, years of profession and his status at the time of the absence. Was he ordained after perpetual profession and incardinated into the institute, or did he enter the institute as a cleric and become incardinated at the time of perpetual profession? What was the reason for his request to live apart from the communal life, and was it given lawfully initially, but became unlawful with the lapse of time and the failure on the part of the competent authorities to address the situation? All of these questions are important to determine the manner in which to approach the case.

If the religious was permitted to remain in this irregular state, and the competent superior did not encourage him to take steps to regularize his canonical status either by returning to the institute or by seeking an indult of departure, then it seems that the onus is on the present competent authorities to meet with the religious and discuss his irregular status. The difficulty here is that the member was led to believe through this inaction that there was no problem; hence, the institute in the person of the major superior is the more responsible agent.

A religious in perpetual vows is incardinated in his institute as a cleric by the reception of the diaconate (c. 266 §2). For such a petitioner (cleric), the indult to leave the institute is not granted until he has been definitively accepted or at least received *ad experimentum* by a diocesan bishop into his diocese (c. 693). It seems that the member in question is willing to depart the institute, but does not want to serve as a diocesan priest, nor does he want to begin the process of laicization.

In 1984, the Congregation for Religious and Secular Institutes (now CICLSAL) offered an option to a cleric who wished to depart his religious institute and for some psychological, moral, or physical reason(s) could not continue in sacred ministry. The cleric had to assure the superior general and the Apostolic See that he would remain celibate, keeping the vow of chastity as a layman in the world (*CLD* XI:92-98).

If the provincial superior meets with this religious, and the religious is willing to depart the institute; the provincial superior can offer his pastoral care by assisting him in this process. The religious should direct his petition to his superior general, indicating in paragraph one: his name, the name of the institute, that he is a cleric in perpetual profession, the nature of his petition (an indult of definitive departure from the institute) with the intention of keeping his clerical promise of celibacy and perfect continence while living as a lay person.

Paragraph two should indicate the reasons for the petition. It would be well to state how he discerned this grave decision. Indicate the period of time away from the institute living as a celibate layperson and a successful at businessman. If he ever discussed his vocation with a spiritual director, canonist, or counselor, he should indicate the same. It may be well to indicate how he appreciated the present provincial superior's attempt to regularize his canonical status and how he has tried since in his absence from the institute to live a life worthy of a member of the Christian faithful. The petition should be dated and signed by him. If he is willing to take the option offered by CICLSAL, he should indicate the same and assure the cardinal prefect in Rome that he intends to continue to live as a layman and observe his promise of clerical celibacy and perfect continence.

The provincial superior should attach a supporting statement, indicating that he has visited the religious and the superior believes that this is the best way to assist him in regularizing his canonical status in the Church. The general superior of the institute should meet with his council and discuss the petition as well as the supporting statement of the provincial superior. They should express their opinions and formulate a written common opinion signed by all (c. 691 §1). It would be well if they were of the opinion that the petitioner would be capable of living as a layman and keeping his promise of celibacy and perfect continence. It is important to note that, if the priest has had problems in the area of chastity with men or women, or if he is interested in marrying or an intimate relationship with another person, male or female, this process is not applicable and should never be recommended by a canonist.

The indult received from CICLSAL would grant the petitioner an indult of departure from the institute with the provision that he would live a celibate, continent life as a lay member of the Christian faithful. The rescript is effective as soon as it is communicated to the petitioner, unless he would reject it in the act of notification (c. 692). This would have to be a formal act of refusal; refusal is most unusual, inasmuch as the religious has had time for prayer, discernment, and consultation before coming to such a grave decision. The man remains a priest forever (*LG* 10). Through the sacrament of orders, he is imprinted with an indelible mark, a character (c. 845 §1). However, with the indult received from CICLSAL, he is dispensed from his obligations in the religious institute and the obligations of sacred ministry. This dispensation includes the canonical obligation of incardination in the clerical religious institute (c. 265); he is permitted to live as a celibate and continent lay person.

When the major superior communicates the contents of the rescript to the religious cleric, it would be salutary to remind him of his formation in religious life and the way that he can witness an exemplary Christian life as a lay person. If the member has no questions and accepts the rescript, the superior can indicate the same on the back of the rescript. The cleric would sign his name and the date, and the superior would sign as the canonical witness. A copy should be given to the petitioner for his records and one kept in the files of the provincial office. If the petitioner lives at a great distance from the provincial house, the superior could advise him of the contents of the rescript by phone, explain its provisions, and ask if he will accept it. The superior would indicate the same on the back of the indult with the time he called the petitioner., sign his name and the date. A copy of the rescript with this notation should be kept in the files of the institutes, and a copy mailed to the petitioner.

Canon 702 §2 provides that one legitimately departing or dismissed from the institute should be dealt with in equity and charity. Most institutes have policies addressing provisions for those leaving the institute. Here there are many variables, since much depends on the patrimony of the member, the means of the institute, the age, health, education and employability of the member. Documents such as the act of cession, the living will or durable power of attorney, and the will of the person should be returned to this person with the indult of departure. All of these were made when he was a member of the institute. If the institute is administering the patrimony of the person, that should be returned in accord with the proper law of the institute. In this case, it would seem the religious would have little claim on the charity of the institute, since he has done well financially during his ten years apart from the institute.

It should be noted that if the priest decides to petition for laicization, the petition would be forwarded by the general superior to the Congregation for the Clergy which is the competent dicastery or curial office in Rome since August 2005.

HELPFUL REFERENCES

- "Canon 691" in *Canon Law Digest* XI:92-98.

- Hill, Richard A. "Departure of a Religious Priest or Deacon." *Review for Religious* 46/6 (Nov./Dec., 1987) 935-938.

- Hynous, David M. "Canon 693 - Dispensation from Vows apart from Priestly Obligations and Celibacy." *Roman Replies and CLSA Advisory Opinions* (1996) 82-85.

- McDonough, Elizabeth. "Communicating an Indult of Departure." *Review for Religious* 51/5 (Sept./Oct. 1992) 782-788.

- Torres, Jesus. "Dispensation from Vows." *Consecrated Life* 18/2 (1995) 82-102.

Case 40

Acceptance of a Clerical Religious *Ad Experimentum*
and Incardination into a Diocese
Canon 693

Case

A clerical religious petitions the bishop for incardination into the diocese. While this priest has served one year in that diocese, the bishop is hesitant to incardinate him immediately. However, he is willing to afford the religious a period of time to test his suitability for secular priesthood. The bishop asks his canonist to advise him regarding the procedure for this experimental period.

QUESTIONS PERTINENT TO THE CASE

1. Is the clerical religious in perpetual profession?
2. Has he discussed his intention with his major superior?
3. What is the reason(s) for his petitioning to depart the religious institute and seek incardination into the diocese?
4. Has the bishop received any communication from the major superior regarding the religious?
5. In what capacity did the priest serve during the year he labored in the diocese; was he missioned by his major superior for that assignment?
6. Is there any priest in the diocese who served with him and could give the diocesan bishop an account of his suitability during that year?
7. Does the bishop have any information regarding his residences and assignments during his life as a religious?
8. Has the major superior communicated to the diocesan bishop in accord with the "Proposed Guidelines on the Assessment of Clergy and Religious for Assignment" offered by the NCCB in November 1993?

THE LAW

Can. 693 If a member is a cleric, an indult is not granted before he finds a bishop who incardinates him in the diocese or at least received him experimentally. If he is received experimentally, he is incardinated into the diocese by the law itself after five years have passed, unless the bishop has refused him.

COMMENTARY

It would be important first to know the canonical status of the clerical religious; is he in temporary or perpetual profession? Canon 693 would not apply to a religious who entered as a cleric and is in temporary profession, since he would be incardinated into the religious institute until his perpetual profession (c. 268 §2). Ordinarily a layman enters and is advanced to perpetual profession in a religious institute before he is ordained to the diaconate and incardinated in the religious institute (c. 266 §2). As a religious, the cleric is accountable to his major superior (provincial or general superior), and it is important that he communicate with the superior regarding his desire to depart the institute and seek incardination into a diocese. It would not seem appropriate for him to communicate with the diocesan bishop and neglect his accountability to his major superior.

Besides interviewing the priest, the diocesan bishop should be in contact with the major superior and request his assessment of the priest for an *ad experimentum* period in the diocese. Was he assigned or did he have his major superior's permission to minister in the diocese the year he served there? The religious' reason for departing the institute and the quality of his community life and apostolic service are important considerations for the diocesan bishop. The major superior should have employed the 1993 NCCB guidelines or similar criteria in his recommendation of the religious for his prior ministry in the diocese. These guidelines, coupled with a recommendation of the religious based on his behavior as a religious would prove helpful to the diocesan bishop in making his decision to admit him *ad experimentum* into the diocese.

If the recommendation of the major superior of the institute is favorable, and the priest has proved suitable during his year of service in the diocese, the diocesan bishop may decide to permit the temporary period of trial. The process consists of a petition written by the religious to the general superior of the institute seeking an indult of departure *ad experimentum* in order to judge his suitability for the vocation of a secular priest. Basically, the petition would be composed of two paragraphs, the one identifying the religious, the institute, the diocese in which the provincilate is located, and his request for an indult of departure from religious life in order to minister in the particular church.

The second paragraph would give his reason(s) for departing religious life and continuing to function as a secular priest. A supporting statement of the provincial superior should accompany the petition of the member along with a letter from the diocesan bishop stating his willingness to receive the priest for the period of experimentation. Finally, a brief *curriculum vitae* of the religious would be included in the communications sent to the general superior. This would simply list the dates of admission, profession, mission assignments, and any offices the religious held during his time in the religious institute.

The four documents would be sent to the general superior who would meet with his council and transmit them along with a personal opinion and the opinion of the council to the competent authority (c. 691 §1). Since most religious institutes of men are of pontifical right, it would seem that the competent authority would be the CICLSAL (c. 691 §2). If that congregation grants the request, the general superior would send a copy of the indult to the provincial superior who in turn would send copies to the diocesan bishop and the religious.

It would be important for the diocesan bishop or his delegate to monitor the priest during the five year period in order to assess his suitability for incardination into the diocese. If the bishop is not pleased with him at any time during this period, the bishop is to advise the major superior, and the religious is to return immediately to his religious institute. Likewise, if the priest decides that the vocation of the secular clergy is unsuitable for him, he is to return to the institute, since he is incardinated in it. If the diocesan bishop is pleased with the religious during this experimental time, he may notify him of his decision to incardinate him into the diocese. When the bishop makes this decision, the indult takes effect, and the religious is incardinated into the diocese and excardinated from his institute. The diocesan bishop should communicate his decision to the provincial superior and CICLSAL. However, if the diocesan bishop fails to act within the five year period, the priest is incardinated into the diocese by the law itself, *ipso iure* (c. 693).

HELPFUL REFERENCES

- NCCB Documentation, "Proposed Guidelines on the Assessment of Clergy and Religious for Assignment." *CLSA Newsletter* (March 1994) 3-4, 6-7.

Rescript for a Religious Cleric Received Experimentally by a Diocesan Bishop

Congregation
for Institutes of Consecrated Life
and Societies of Apostolic Life

Prot. n. _____

Most Holy Father

The priest _____ of the (Order or Congregation)_____ implores Your Holiness for an indult to depart his institute for the reasons provided. The Ordinary _____ in _____ intends to receive him into the diocese for a period of experimentation in accord with canon 693 of the Code of Canon Law.

_____

The Congregation for Institutes of Consecrated Life and Societies of Apostolic Life, having heard the opinion of the Procuratrix General of the institute and being attentive to the letters of acceptance for the experimental period from the Ordinary _____ in _____ , the same, having agreed in accord with his prudent judgment and conscience to grant the petitioner an indult of exclaustration during the experimental period, he lays aside the external form of the religious habit and complies with all that is to be observed in accord with the norm of canon 687 in the Code of Canon Law. If it should happen during the experimental period that the same Ordinary, having warned the Superior, rejects the petitioner, he is to return immediately to the cloister.

The time of experimentation having been completed, however, or if he is definitively received before that time, the petitioner having agreed to the sustenance provided, remains secularized and absolved from the vows in the institute he is leaving; by that fact he is incardinated in the diocese of _____ in _____ in accord with the norm of canons 265, 267, 269 of the Code of Canon Law.

Anything contrary to the above does not stand.

Given in Vatican City _____ .

_____
Secretary

_____
Undersecretary

204

Case 41

Ipso Facto Dismissal and Readmission to a Clerical Religious Institute
Canons 694; 194 §1, 3°; 1044 §1, 3°; 1041, 3°; 1394 §1

Case

A gentleman makes an appointment with the provincial superior of a clerical religious institute. He advises the superior that he had been in the institute, attempted marriage and was dismissed. He recognized that he had made a grave mistake but believed he had committed himself to the woman, and she developed cancer three years after the attempted marriage. Recently his wife died resultant from the cancer, and he wanted to know if there was any possibility of his return to sacred ministry as a member of the institute.

QUESTIONS PERTINENT TO THE CASE

1. How long had the man been in the religious institute prior to the attempted marriage?
2. Is the institute of diocesan or pontifical right?
3. Was he in temporary or perpetual profession?
4. Was he ordained in the institute after perpetual profession and incardinated into it following ordination to the diaconate?
5. What was the quality of his life while in the institute? Had he lived well with his brothers, accepted assignments, and performed them with competence?
6. How long had he lived in the invalid marriage?
7. What was the quality of his life with the woman; what did he do to support both of them during the attempted marriage?
8. Are there any children resultant from the marriage; how old are they? What is their attitude toward their father returning to the institute?
9. What has been the quality of his spiritual life during these years; how is he coping with the death of his wife?
10. Can he give any character references for his time away from religious life, e.g., his pastor, an employer, etc.?
11. Why does he want to return to the religious institute he left?

12. How old is the priest; is he in good health; does he have an familial or financial debts that are outstanding at this time?
13. How does he think the members of the institute will respond to his return?
14. If he has been out a considerable number of years, does he recognize the institute has changed considerably since his departure?
15. Is there anyone dependent on him for emotional and monetary support?

THE LAW

Can. 694 §1. A member must be held as *ipso facto* dismissed from an institute who:
    1° has defected notoriously from the Catholic faith;
    2° has contracted marriage or attempted it, even only civilly.
    §2. In these cases, after the proofs have been collected, the major superior with the council is to issue without any delay a declaration of fact so that the dismissal is established juridically.

Can. 194 §1. The following are removed from an ecclesiastical office by the law itself:
    3° a cleric who has attempted marriage even if only civilly.
    §2. The removal mentioned in nn. 2 and 3 can be enforced only if it is established by the declaration of a competent authority.

Can. 1044 §1. The following are irregular for the exercise of orders received:
    3° a person who has committed a delict mentioned in can. 1041, nn. 3, 4, 5, 6.

Can. 1041, 3° a person who has attempted marriage, even only civilly, while either impeded personally from entering marriage by a matrimonial bond, sacred orders, or a public perpetual vow of chastity, or with a woman bound by a valid marriage or restricted by the same type of vow;

Can. 1394 §1. Without prejudice to the prescript of can. 194, §1, n.3, a cleric who attempts marriage, even if only civilly, incurs a *latae sententiae* suspension. If he does not repent after being warned and continues to give scandal, he can be punished gradually by privations or even by dismissal from the clerical state.

COMMENTARY

If a canonist is assisting the provincial superior with the case, it is important to know the kind of clerical institute, the status of the religious at the time of the attempted marriage and the length of time spent in both the marriage and the religious institute. It would be good to know, too, how the attempted marriage came about, and if there was scandal resulting from the same. In other words, a profile of the religious is important and usually requested by the Congregation for the Clergy (CC) If the quality of life in the institute was poor prior to the marriage, i.e., he did not interrelate well with other members in the institute or had serious problems in his ministerial assignments, then it would seem the provincial superior should proceed with great caution. It may be that better to discourage such a person from the very beginning and forestall future problems both for the institute and for him.

Second, it would be well to have some sense of the quality of the marriage. The marriage was invalid in church law due to two diriment impediments, sacred orders, and the public perpetual vow of chastity in a religious institute (cc. 1087 and 1088). With the death of his wife, the civil bond ended. It does speak well for the man that he honored the commitment he made to the woman, even though he recognized he had made a grave mistake. The provincial superior should inquire as to the quality of their life together, if there were children, and how they supported themselves during those years. How did his wife die, and were there children by the marriage. If he cared for her during her illness, this would again speak well for his responsibility to the commitment he made. If there are children, he should continue to provide spiritual, emotional, and financial support for them until they reach the age of majority. It would seem that no consideration should be given to readmitting one who has such grave responsibility towards children, parents, or other close relatives.

If the man has no children, had a reasonably good relationship with his wife of twelve years, has led a decent Christian life insofar as possible, has been gainfully employed, offers character references, shows genuine remorse for his defection, then it would seem that serious consideration can be given to assisting his readmission. It would be less than honest if the provincial superior did not advise him that he may experience some *admiratio* from some members at his return. However, in large institutes this can often be handled by assigning the readmitted priest to a province different than the one to which he was attached before his dismissal. Care should be taken to make certain he does not return to the same area wherein he ministered or where he lived during his marriage.

If the interview goes well, and the provincial has reason to believe that the priest can be rehabilitated, the irregularity caused by the attempted marriage and seems to be public has to be removed. Since dispensation from this irregularity is reserved to the Apostolic See (c. 1047 §3), and the supreme moderator would eventually petition the CC regarding this dispensation. The same superior can also request the removal of the *latae sententiae* suspension incurred by the priest in attempting marriage (c. 1394 §1). While the major superior of the religious institute could remit this latter unreserved and undeclared *latae sententiae* suspension, the CC can do both at once.

Since readmission to the institute provided in canon 690 §1 pertains to those who have legitimately left the institute after completing the novitiate or after profession, the supreme moderator would also have to request permission from the CC permission for him to be readmitted to the institute without repeating the novitiate but with a suitable probation period prior to temporary profession in accord with canons 655 and 657. If a priest has been away from the institute a number of years, the Apostolic See requires that he take a renewal course in theology. However, if this priest has demonstrated exemplary quality of life both during his time in the institute and in his relationship with the woman during the three years in the invalid marriage, it would seem that the supreme moderator could request a dispensation to reduce the three year period required in temporary profession.

HELPFUL REFERENCES

- Congregation for the Clergy. "Criteria for Rehabilitation." and "Points to be Considered in the Presentation of Requests for Dispensation from the Irregularity 'Ad Ordines Exercendos' Incurred after Attempted Marriage by Priests and Deacons (Canon 1044)." Both the criteria and points are published in *Roman Replies* (2001) 22-26.

- Woestman, William. *The Sacrament of Orders and the Clerical State*. Ottawa: St. Paul University, 2001: 205-217.

Case 42

Dismissal of a Clerical Religious from a Religious Institute
Canon 696

Case

A religious received a first canonical warning from his provincial superior due
to his irregular absence from the institute and asks for canonical advice. He had
been sent to the United States to study and complete the requirements for a
doctorate in science. The provincial superior wants to assign him to teach in the
university in his native country. The religious has completed the degree and wants
to continue his scientific research in the United States and minister in a parish
during the weekends. What issues should be addressed with this religious?

QUESTIONS PERTINENT TO THE CASE

1. Is the institute of pontifical or diocesan right?
2. In which country is the province of the religious, the generalate?
3. Is the religious in perpetual profession; was he ordained before admission to the
   institute or after he made perpetual profession in the institute?
4. Did the priest understand that his vow of obedience leaves him open to
   whatever service the legitimate superiors ask of him in keeping with his gifts
   and the needs of the Church?
5. When did he complete the requirements for the degree, and how long has he
   been in the United States contrary to the wishes of the provincial superior?
6. How has he been sustaining himself with room, board, and other necessities
   during this period of unlawful absence from the institute?
7. Does the canonical warning have the five essential elements required, and is it
   based on six months illegitimate absence from the institute; did the religious
   reply to the warning?
8. Does he serve in any diocese at present; has he any prospects for continuing his
   sacred ministry with his scientific research?
9. Are there any prospects for his obtaining grants to continue his scientific
   research; has he ready access to the materials, etc. he needs to do the research?
10. In his opinion, which seems to be the higher priority in his life, his vocation as

a clerical religious or his profession as a research scientist?

11. What is the priest's legal status in the United States; does he have an F-1 visa as a student in this country?

12. Has he pursued the non-immigrant R-1 status in order to work in the United States?

THE LAW

Can. 696 §1. A member can also be dismissed for other causes provided that they are grave, external, imputable, and juridically proven such as: habitual neglect of the obligation of consecrated life; repeated violations of the sacred bonds; stubborn disobedience to the legitimate prescripts of superiors in a grave matter; grave scandal arising from the culpable behavior of the member; stubborn upholding or diffusion of doctrines condemned by the magisterium of the Church; public adherence to ideologies infected by materialism or atheism; the illegitimate absence mentioned in can. 665, §2, lasting six months; other causes of similar gravity which the proper law of the institute may determine.

Can. 693 If a member is a cleric, an indult (of departure) is not granted before he finds a bishop who incardinates him in the diocese or at least receives him experimentally. If he is received experimentally, he is incardinated into the diocese by the law itself after five years have passed, unless the bishop has refused him.

COMMENTARY

One must be extremely sensitive to this priest who is dedicated to his scholarly research in the United States. Undoubtedly, he has met with opportunities in his scientific studies that he did not have in his own country. Still, he did make a commitment to a religious institute through his profession to be open to being sent for the needs of the Church in accord with the nature, spirit, and goals of the religious institute. To that end, the institute has permitted him to study in the United States and financed his education, enabling him to complete a doctorate. Now, his major superior anticipates his teaching skills in the university of his own country. He has received his degree and is already in an irregular status of absence from the institute (c. 665 §2). Certainly, his refusal to return to his native country and teach is a major disappointment for the major superior and provincial council.

The canonist should assist him in facing the realities of his life. He is at once a priest, a religious, and a scientist. What are his priorities, and how does he visualize his life's journey? He should realize that in providing him with an education, the institute had expectations of his serving the Church; he vowed obedience to the legitimate commands of superiors to do just that. This first canonical warning resulting from his refusal to return to his country and teach reflects his failure to

210

comply with the obligations of his religious profession. Another concern would be his legal status in the country; has he an F-1 non-immigrant visa to study? He will have to address this with the appropriate civil authorities if he decides to stay in the United States and seek an R-1 status as a worker. It would seem he needs assurance of a position and a sponsor for the latter.

While the canonist seeks to learn the cleric's priorities, he or she could recommend that he try to abort the distasteful process of dismissal by petitioning for an indult of departure from his religious institute if his mind is made up to continue scientific research. In this way, he will avoid the stigma of dismissal and continue his research if that is his priority. However, he should be made realize that if he wishes to continue sacred ministry, the indult of departure is not given unless he finds a benevolent bishop who will accept him *ad experimentum*. It is not too likely that a bishop will admit into a diocese a priest who can only guarantee weekend ministry. Cut off from the financial assistance of the institute, he will have to rely on his own resources for sustenance. Can he sustain himself while doing research; will he address his legal status?

All of this should be presented to the religious, and he should be encouraged to bring his discernment to prayer, to seek spiritual direction, and to recognize that a decision on his part to move in the direction of scientific research would necessarily curtail his availability for sacred ministry in a diocese. While canon 693 provides that a cleric is not granted an indult of departure before he finds a bishop who incardinates him in the diocese or receives him experimentally, CICLSAL has granted indults of departure to clerics without this provision if they have no intention of continuing sacred ministry and promise to live a celibate, continent life as lay persons in the Church. However, a petition for such an indult should be accompanied by the supporting opinion of the superior general and council of the religious institute.

HELPFUL REFERENCES

- Office for the Pastoral Care of Migrants and Refugees of the NCCB. *Guidelines for Receiving Pastoral Ministers in the United States.* Washington, D.C.: USCC, Inc., 1999.

SAMPLE

FIRST CANONICAL WARNING

Dear Father_____,

On _____, I met with my council in accord with canon 697 of the Code of Canon Law and decided to initiate the dismissal process in issuing you this first canonical warning. Your failure to abide by its mandate will result in dismissal from out religious institute.

For the past seven years you have been assigned to the United States of America to complete doctoral studies in science. Having received your degree on _____, you have remained nine months in an irregular absence in that country. You have failed to return to our province and assume the responsibility of teaching in the University of _____. This places you in the irregular canonical status of an unlawful absence beyond six months and subject to dismissal in accord with canon 696 §1 of the Code of Canon Law.

In virtue of your vow of obedience, I command you to return to this country and your major superior in order to accept a residence and an assignment by me by _____ .. This allows you two months to pack and ready yourself to depart the United States. If you need fare for travel or any other need, please notify our provincial treasurer, informing him of the amount.

You have a right to defend yourself in this matter either to me or to our general superior, Very Rev. _____ in Rome in accord with canon 698.

In the meantime, together with the provincial council, I pray for you that you come to recognize the beauty of the commitment you made to God through your religious profession as a member of our institute and return to our province and the ministry of teaching.

_____   _____
Date   Provincial Superior

Note: If the provincial superior issues a second canonical warning, it repeats the content of the first one and must include the same five essential elements: 1. the offense committed, 2. the way to remedy the situation, 3. the right of the member to defense, 4. the time within which the member must comply with the order, and 5. the threat of dismissal for failure to comply with the order of the major superior. Nothing of content is to be added or changed with the exception of the new date of the second warning, the fact that it is the second warning since the member failed to respond or his defense to the first canonical warning was inadequate. Finally, the time within which he has to comply will have to be adjusted in the second warning.

Case 43

Confirmation of a Decree of Dismissal
from a Religious Institute of Pontifical Right
Canon 700

Case

The general superior of a religious institute of pontifical right is about to petition the Congregation for Consecrated Life for a confirmation of a decree of dismissal issued by the same moderator for one of the members of the institute. What would be some documents that should be enclosed with the petition as acts of the case and transmitted to Rome?

THE LAW

Can. 700 A decree of dismissal does not have effect unless it has been confirmed by the Holy See, to which the decree and all the acts must be transmitted; if it concerns an institute of diocesan right, confirmation belongs to the bishop of the diocese where the house to which the religious has been attached is situated. To be valid, however, the decree must indicate the right which the dismissed possesses to make recourse to the competent authority within ten days from receiving notification. The recourse has suspensive effect.

COMMENTARY

Because the vocation of a religious and the rights and obligations of both the member and the institute are involved in a dismissal from the institute, the CICLSAL, or a diocesan bishop in the case of a religious institute of diocesan right, is scrupulously careful in examining and determining the merits of such cases. Confirmation of decrees of dismissal pertain only to mandatory (c. 695) and facultative (c. 696) dismissals. If the case involves an *ipso facto* dismissal (c. 694), there is no confirmation of the declaration of the fact of dismissal (c. 694 §2). In such cases, the member's action effects the dismissal, and the major superior with the council collects the proofs and declares the fact of dismissal.

213

In a mandatory dismissal (c. 695), the following documentation should be included with the petition for confirmation:

1. A *curriculum vitae* of the member (dates of birth, admission to the institute, temporary and perpetual professions, assignments or offices held in the institute, any other canonical facts, e.g., transfer, exclaustration, readmission).

2. A statement indicating that the member was confronted with the delict committed (cc. 1397, 1398, 1395) and the facts and proofs of his or her imputability. The statement should further advise that the member was advised of the right to self-defense which could be submitted to the immediate major superior or the supreme moderator (cc. 695 §2, 698). All of this may have been accomplished in a meeting of the major superior and vicar general or another councilor with the member. A written account of the meeting should be dated, signed, and notarized (c. 695 §2).

3. The written defense of the member signed and dated; if there is not defense, this should be noted by the major superior.

4. The results of the collegial vote of the general council (supreme moderator and four councilors) as described in c. 699 §1.

5. If the councilors were less than four, the process employed to procure the additional member(s) for the collegial voting (c. 699 §1) should be described.

6. The decree of dismissal submitted for confirmation should detail in summary fashion the grave offense of the member, the facts and proofs of the offense, as well as the member's imputability and inadequate self-defense. It should further state the applicable law and the results of the collegial vote of the general council for dismissal. The decree must state the right of the member to take recourse to the Congregation for Consecrated Life within ten days from receiving the decree of dismissal. The dismissed member should be made to understand that such recourse has suspensive effect (c. 700).

If the dismissal is a facultative or discretionary one as described in canon 696, all of the above is submitted to the same Congregation or diocesan bishop with the following included:

1. A record of the minutes of the council meeting showing that the major superior has heard the council regarding the decision to proceed with dismissal (c. 697).

2. Copies of the two canonical warnings presented to the member about to be dismissed. These warnings should include: 1) a statement of the grave offense

committed, 2) the remedial action to be taken by the member, 3) the right of the member to self-defense, 4) the time within which to reply to the warning (at least fifteen days), and 5) the threat of dismissal if the warning is not heeded. (c. 697, 2°). If the warnings were by registered mail to the member, proof of registered mail should be attached and some indication of the reply or lack of response by the member.

3. A record of the minutes of the council meeting showing that the major superior with the council decided that incorrigibility was evident and the defense(s) of the member were insufficient (c. 697, 3°).

4. A statement of the major superior indicating that all of the acts signed by him or her and a notary were sent to the supreme moderator at least fifteen days after the last warning (c. 697, 3°).

All of the above are extremely important, since failure to observe the correct canonical procedure in a dismissal can lead to CICLSAL's refusal to confirm the decree.

HELPFUL REFERENCES

- Holland, Sharon. "Chapter VI Separation of Members from the Institute (cc. 684-704):" 870-871. *New Commentary on the Code of Canon Law.* Edited by John P. Beal, James A. Coriden, and Thomas J. Green. New York/Mahwah: Paulist Press, 2000.

DECREE OF DISMISSAL

The undersigned General Superior, having proceeded collegially with the General Council on (date) to weigh the proofs, arguments and defenses in the case, and in the same manner having moved to a decision by secret ballot, decrees that Sister NN, a (perpetually) professed member of the (Congregation) is hereby dismissed for the following reasons.

According to the proper law of this Institute (Const. nn.) And the law of the Church (cc.) religious are obliged to _____ . Canon law also recognizes that failure in this matter constitutes a cause for dismissal, stating among other causes "_____ ."
(c. 696 §1).

In the present case, despite various efforts to correct the situation, including two canonical warnings issued (date/date) Sister NN has persisted in the behavior which violates the above religious obligations. (Brief resumé of factual violation which merit dismissal in the case).

This decree takes effect following its confirmation by the Holy See. Sister NN then has ten days, following receipt of notification of the confirmed decree, within which she may have recourse to the Holy See.

_____
General Superior

Date:_____

Seal

_____
General Secretary

1. For validity, there must be a council of four in addition to the General Superior, but the decision is made by secret collegial vote. Either the Decree or the cover letter or an excerpt from the Council minutes should make clear that the required number were present and whether the vote was unanimous.

2. For validity of the Decree, it must contain a summary of the cause of dismisal in fact–the actions of the religious, and in law showing that the violations were

contrary to universal and proper law and are of a type an gravity considered in laws, grounds for dismissal.

3. For validity, the Decree must contain notice that the religious has ten days from the receipt of notification within which to appeal.

4. If the case involves the causes in can. 695, mandatory dismissal, there are no canonical warnings, but rather an emphasis on proofs of fact and imputability.

Case 44

Communicating an Indult of Departure and a Decree of Dismissal:
Acceptance or Rejection
Canons 692 and 701

Case 1

Frequently a major superior will inquire as to the process for communicating an indult of departure when the religious is not present in the diocese or state, and it would prove a hardship to set up an appointment for the religious. At times, too, a religious will not accept the indult until he or she is satisfied that the financial assistance given by his or her religious institute in accord with canon 702 §2 is adequate. How should the canonist advise the major superior?

QUESTIONS PERTINENT TO THE CASE

1. Did the religious voluntarily request the indult of departure?
2. Has the major superior received the indult from the bishop of the diocese of assignment in the case of a diocesan right institute, or from CICLSAL in the case of an institute of pontifical right?

THE LAW

> Can. 692 Unless it has been rejected by the member in the act of notification, an indult of departure granted legitimately and made known to the member entails by the law itself dispensation from the vows and from all the obligations arising from profession.

> Can. 702 §1. Those who depart from a religious institute legitimately or have been dismissed from it legitimately can request nothing from the institute for any work done in it.
> §2. Nevertheless, the institute is to observe equity and the charity of the gospel toward a member who is separated from it.

It would not seem that the religious who has petitioned for the indult of departure for "the gravest of causes considered before the Lord" (c. 691 §1) will reject it when it is made known to him or her. However, even with the notification of the indult, the religious is free to refuse it. If the indult is rejected, the religious must return immediately to the religious institute and resume common life and other obligations of canonical religious life assumed at religious profession (c. 654).

It is important for the major superior to recognize that acceptance of the indult of departure is not contingent upon the member's satisfaction with the financial assistance he or she is given. If the religious rejects the indult, he or she remains a religious and is bound to the obligations assumed at religious profession. It should be remembered also that the obligation on the part of the religious institute in canon 702 §2 is one of equity and charity, not justice. Most institutes have policies in this matter, and provision is given after consideration of the age and health of the individual departing, the education received in the institute and the corresponding capability for gainful employment, personal patrimony or other temporal goods that one departing a religious congregation may have, and the ability of the institute to give the charitable monetary sum. But a religious cannot refuse to accept the indult of departure and use acceptance as a "bargaining chip" for a desired sum of money. It must be recalled to such a member that at religious profession he or she gave a total gift of self to the Lord in service to His people in accord with the nature and purpose of the institute. That promise made at profession endures while one remains a religious. Likewise, the departing religious should be reminded of the effects of the vow of poverty made at first profession:

> Can. 668 §3. Whatever a religious acquires through personal effort or by reason of the institute, the religious acquires for the institute. Whatever accrues to a religious in any way by reason of pension, subsidy, or insurance is acquired for the institute unless proper law states otherwise.

It is the opinion of this canonist that some record should be made in the files of the institute of the fact that the indult was communicated to and accepted by the religious. Therefore, the religious: 1) can be notified that the indult has arrived from the ecclesiastical authority and asked to come for a meeting with the major superior at a mutually agreeable time so that the indult can be explained; or 2) the religious can be telephoned and advised that the indult has arrived and an explanation of its effects given over the phone.

In both cases, the religious would receive two copies of the indult, the one to be signed on the back, indicating acceptance and dated, the other to be kept for his or her own file. If institutes have been careful when religious make perpetual profession, notification should be sent to the parish of baptism (c. 535 §2). Since perpetual profession in a religious institute is a diriment impediment to marriage (c. 1088), a copy of the indult of departure would prove the freedom of the person to marry. Also, the major superior would have a record of the acceptance of the rescript for the files of the institute. If this has not been done in the past by major superiors, the fact that the religious did not formally reject the indult he or she voluntarily petitioned would seem to be sufficient. Notification should be made in the files that the indult was communicated to the religious on a particular date and not rejected.

Case 2

At times a religious dismissed from the institute will not "accept" the decree of dismissal until he or she receives what he or she believes to be adequate financial assistance from the religious institute. How should the canonist advise the major superior in this situation?

QUESTIONS PERTINENT TO CASE 2

1. Was the decree of dismissal confirmed by the competent ecclesiastical authority before it was communicated to the religious?
2. When the decree of dismissal was communicated to the member, did it indicate the right of that member to take recourse to the competent authority within ten days from receiving notification?
3. Did the religious make recourse, and has a response come from the competent ecclesiastical authority?

THE LAW

Can. 700 A decree of dismissal does not have effect unless it has been confirmed by the Holy See, to which the decree and all the acts must be transmitted; if it concerns an institute of diocesan right, confirmation belongs to the bishop of the diocese where the house to which the religious has been attached is situated. To be valid, however, the decree must indicate the right which the dismissed possesses to make recourse to the competent authority within ten days from receiving notification. The recourse has suspensive effect.

Can. 701 By legitimate dismissal, vows as well as the rights and obligations deriving from profession cease *ipso facto*. Nevertheless, if the member is a cleric, he cannot exercise sacred orders until he finds a bishop who receives him into the diocese after an appropriate probation according to the norm of can. 693 or at least permits him to exercise sacred orders.

COMMENTARY

The important thing here is to be certain that the dismissal is valid: 1) it has been confirmed by the competent ecclesiastical authority and 2) the decree stated clearly that the religious had the right to take recourse within ten days from the act of notification. If the religious did take recourse, the major superior must wait to hear the results of the same. If the religious did not make recourse, then the legitimate dismissal is effective, since it was not a voluntary petition on the part of the religious, but a collegial decision of the general council, issued by the supreme moderator (c. 699 §1) and confirmed by ecclesiastical authority (c. 700).

Unlike the indult of voluntary departure, the refusal of the religious to accept a a decree of dismissal has no effect, since a legitimate dismissal *ipso facto* dispenses from the vows as well as all other rights and obligations deriving from religious profession. While the religious institute is obliged to deal with the religious with equity and charity as provided in canon 702 §2 for religious who legitimately depart and those legitimately dismissed, the religious has no choice but to accept the effects of dismissal from the institute.

HELPFUL REFERENCES

- See the commentaries on the canons cited above in Holland, I.H.M., Sharon."Chapter VI Separation of Members from the Institute (cc. 684-704):" 801-803, 869-872. *New Commentary on the Code of Canon Law*. Edited by John P Beal, James A. Coriden, and Thomas J. Green. New York/Mahwah: Paulist Press, 2000.

Case 45

Equity and Charity Toward a Separated Member
Canon 702 §2

Case

The provincial superior of a clerical religious institute calls a canonist. He is upset over a letter he received from a civil attorney. A priest who has been absent from the institute for nine years (three years on exclaustration and six years in an irregular canonical status) has decided to seek definitive separation. The member wants the institute to give him a substantial sum of money and retirement benefits as he leaves the institute. He has hired the attorney and threatens to take the institute to court if the provincial superior does not acquiesce to his demand. What advice should the canonist offer to the provincial superior?

QUESTIONS PERTINENT TO THE CASE

1. Is the institute of pontifical or diocesan right?
2. Is the institute a congregation (simple profession) or an order (solemn profession)?
3. How long has the member been in perpetual profession?
4. How old is he; is he in good health?
5. What apostolic service did the member perform prior to his exclaustration?
6. What is his general background, his life in the institute, his educational background?
7. Why did he petition for the indult of exclaustration; was there any follow-up during or at the end of the three year period of exclaustration?
8. Has he offered any reason for requesting this definitive departure from the institute?
9. What is the policy of the institute for the need of the members definitively departing or legitimately dismissed?
10. Has the institute been consistent in following the policy with departing members?

Canon 668 §1. Before first profession, members are to cede the administration of their goods to whomever they prefer and, unless the constitutions state otherwise, are to make dispositions freely for their use and revenue. Moreover, at least before perpetual profession, they are to make a will which is to be valid also in civil law.

§2. To change these dispositions for a just cause and to place any act regarding temporal goods, they need the permission of the superior competent according to the norm of proper law.

§3. Whatever a religious acquires through personal effort or by reason of the institute, the religious acquires for the institute. Whatever accrues to a religious in any way by reason of pension, subsidy, or insurance is acquired for the institute unless proper law states otherwise.

§4. A person who must renounce fully his or her goods due to the nature of the institute is to make that renunciation before perpetual profession in a form valid, as far as possible, even in civil law; it is to take effect from the day of profession. A perpetually professed religious who wishes to renounce his or her goods either partially or totally according to the norm of proper law and with the permission of the supreme moderator is to do the same.

§5. A professed religious who has renounced his or her goods fully due to the nature of the institute loses the capacity of acquiring and possessing and therefore invalidly places acts contrary to the vow of poverty. Moreover, whatever accrues to the professed after renunciation belongs to the institute according to the norm of proper law.

Can. 702 §1. Those who depart from a religious institute legitimately or have been dismissed from it legitimately can request nothing from the institute for any work done in it.

§2. Nevertheless, the institute is to observe equity and the charity of the gospel toward a member who is separated from it.

COMMENTARY

It would be important for the canonist first to have a good knowledge of the religious institute: is it of pontifical or diocesan right; is the profession simple (c. 668 §1) or solemn (c. 668 §4, §5); its capability to address the needs of its members, both the members and those legitimately separated from the institute. Next the canonist should have a good profile of the member: his age and health, time spent in the institute, education and apostolic service, and the reason(s) for petitioning for exclaustration (c. 686), for the irregular absence (c. 665 §2), and his reason for the petition for definitive departure (c. 691-693).

Another important aspect would be what he has been doing during the nine years away from the institute. He remains a priest; is he practicing sacred orders;

how is he sustaining himself over this extended period of time? What work is he presently doing, and how has his education in the institute prepared him for it? Has he maintained any contact with the institute over these nine years, either with the authorities or friends in the institute? In keeping with this time away, it would be important to see what form of profession the priest made in the institute. If he belongs to a religious institute that requires a renunciation of personal goods prior to perpetual profession (c. 668 §4, §5), the priest has not only renounced what he had at that time, but any claim to personal goods in the future. The priest may be shocked to learn that if he belongs to an order with solemn vows, his earnings belong to the religious institute, since he is still a member of the institute wherein he renounced ownership. Oftentimes religious neglect to consider that as long as they remain in such an irregular canonical status (c. 665 §2), they remain members of the institute.

Next, it should be explained to the provincial superior that the member, whether in simple or solemn profession has no claim in justice to anything from the institute (c. 702 §1). Any assistance the institute offers as he departs is given in accord with charity and equity as prescribed in the universal law (c. 702 §2). The theology behind this norm is that a person gives himself as a total donation to God in service to his people. The service of a religious is offered as pure gift freely given in a life of charity.

Civil lawyers do not always understand the canonical provisions based on religious vocation, and attempt to assist the religious as if he were one leaving a profession in accord with the years in religious life. There are significant differences in canonical norms regarding charitable assistance to departing members and just severance requirements in secular professions.

Another practical issue is the priest's demand for retirement benefits. The retirement provisions of religious institutes are clearly marked and reserved funds for the members. Major superiors and financial officers in charge of such reserved funds must be careful to avoid violating the provisions of the fund. Most often the beneficiaries are clearly the members of the institute; to break this contract by giving pensions to those outside the membership could lead to a loss of the retirement plan.

The best situation here would be for the priest, the civil attorney, the canonist, and the provincial superior to meet and have the canonist explain to both the civil attorney and the religious the provisions of his vow of poverty in the institute, as well as the canonical norm and policy of the institute for departing members. While most religious institutes have policies and follow them as closely as possible, there are always individual differences that must be attended. For example, some members leave at an advanced age having served the Church for a great period of time. The departing member may not be in the best of health, and employment may be difficult to find. Likewise, some religious have little or no patrimony simply because they entered at an early age or entered a religious order which required renunciation of personal goods. On the other hand, the priest may be in good health, have received a fine education in the institute, has a fine position, and lives

225

an above average lifestyle. The institute may have secured Social Security benefits for its members; and therefore, the priest would have access to it. Some institutes have put aside a charitable trust from which to offer monetary assistance to those departing. All of these considerations must be taken into consideration. But money is never given simply due to the pressure of a civil attorney or the demands of a member failing to understand the obligations and implications of the vow of poverty he or she once made.

This case focused primarily on canon 702. It should be remembered that this is a priest as well as a religious. If he plans to seek incardination in a diocese and continue sacred ministry, he must find a benevolent bishop in accord with canon 693. If he plans to live as a lay person, then he must seek laicization as prescribed in canons 290, 3°; 291; or petition for an indult of departure with a promise to live a chaste celibate life as a lay person (c. 691).

HELPFUL REFERENCES

- Holland, Sharon. "Policies when a Member Leaves the Religious Institute."*Informationes SCRIS* 26/2 (2000) 125-138.

- McDermott, Rose. "Canon 702 §2: Equity and Charity to Separated Members." *CLSA Proceedings of the Fifty-Second Annual Convention* (Oct. 15-18, 1990) 120-133.

- Ricceri, Don Luigi. "The Economic Subsidy to be Granted Religious Who Leave their Institute." *Consecrated Life* ½ (1975) 161-170.

- Welch, Madeline, O.S.U. and Peter Campbell, C.F.X. "Provisions for Departing Members." *Bulletin on Issues of Religious Law* 12 (Fall 1996) 1-16.

c., cc., Can.	canon(s)
CCEO	*Code of Canons of the Eastern Churches*
CLD	*Canon Law Digest*
CLSA Proceedings	*Canon Law Society of America Proceedings*
CICLSAL	Congregation for Institutes of Consecrated Life and Secular Institutes
CLSGB&I Newsletter	*Canon Law Society of Great Britain & Ireland Newsletter*
CMSM	Conference of Major Superiors of Men
Informationes SCRIS	Information Bulletin Sacred Congregation for Religious and Secular Institutes
LCWR	Leadership Conference of Religious Women
LG	*Lumen Gentium* (21 November 1964) Dogmatic Constitution on the Church
NACPA	National Association of Church Personnel Administrators
NATRI	National Association of Treasurers of Religious Institutes
NCCB	National Conference of Catholic Bishops
PC	*Perfectae caritatis* (28 October 1965) Decree on the Up-to-date Renewal of Religious Life
Rom.	St. Paul's letter to the People of Rome
SCDW	Sacred Congregation for Divine Worship
USA	United States of America
USCC	United States Catholic Conference
USCCB	United States Conference of Catholic Bishops
USIG Bulleten	*Union of Superiors International General Bulletin*
VC	*Vita Consecrata*
17CIC	*1917 Codex Iuris Canonici*

ABOUT THE AUTHOR

Sister Rose McDermott, SSJ is a Sister of St. Joseph. She has been actively involved in the ministry of canon law in a variety of settings and ministries. She has contributed most especially in the field of education, beginning in high school and parochial schools in three archdioceses (Philadelphia, Newark and Washington, DC and two dioceses, Camden and Harrisburg). Sister Rose received a Bachelor's degree in English and History at Chestnut Hill College in 1969 and an M.A, in Religious Studies from Providence College in Rhode Island in 1974. She earned a doctorate in canon law from the Catholic University of America in 1979.

Since receiving that degree our author has been involved in a variety of teaching positions in the field of canon law, including classes in Canon Law for the Laity at Boston College and Trinity College in Washington; has also taught in seminary formation programs at Mary Immaculate Seminary (Vincentian Seminary) in Northampton, Pennsylvania, St. Charles Archdiocesan Seminary in Philadelphia, Pennsylvania, and seminarians from Theological College and Washington Theological Consortium at Catholic University.

In addition, Sister Rose has served as a canonist for several Institutes of Consecrated Life and Societies of Apostolic Life, and she has served as a consultant for many bishops, chancellors and Vicars in promoting Consecrated Life.

Our recipient presently serves as a Consultor for the Congregation for Institutes of Consecrated Life and Societies of Apostolic Life, an appointment renewed in 2000 for five more years.

Our author has published articles on consecrated life in *Review for Religious, The Jurist, Commentarium pro Religiosi, Studia Canonica, Bulletin de Saint-Sulpice,* and *Jeevadhara.* She has contributed articles to the *New Catholic Encyclopedia* as well as to the commentaries on the canons on consecrated life in *The Code of Canon Law: A text and Commentary* (1985) and *New Commentary on the Code of Canon Law* (2000).

Sister Rose McDermott is presently Associate Professor of Canon Law at The Catholic University of America in Washington, DC, where in addition to the work she does with licentiate students, she continues to be available to assist any and all who call her as a consultant on matters of Consecrated Life and other issues. She once wrote "in our class on consecrated life, we need to be familiar with public juridic persons, church governance, elections, postulations, and ecclesiastical

229

offices in book 1; associations of the faithful, Roman curial offices, diocesan structure and the authority of bishops in book 2; catechetics, missionary activity, and Catholic education in book 3; the faculties of clerical religious for sacred ministry in book 4; temporal goods, their administration and alienation in book 5; sanctions dismissing or mandating the dismissal of a religious in book 6; and the process for recourse against administrative decrees with the removal of a religious pastor in book 7."

Sister Rose has been a member of the Canon Law Society of America since 1977, serving on the Board of Governors from 1980 – 1982. Since 1991, she has been Assistant Editor of the yearly publication of *Roma Replies and CLSA Advisory Opinions* Sister Rose McDermott is the recipient of the 2002 Canon Law Society of America Role of Law Award.

bishop's review of proposed changes to Constitutions of institution of diocesan
        right, 45–48
    brother elected as major superior of clerical institute in violation of, 89–91
    province, changes to allow institute of pontifical right to erect, 17–21
    universal suffrage for perpetually professed members at chapters, change of
        Constitution to allow, 108–109
contracts or agreements or contracts between institutes and dioceses
    apostolates, agreements regarding, 161–164
    parishes, clerical institutes taking charge of, 3–8
councilors of major superior, advice and consent of, 101–103

D
departure from institute. *See* dismissal or departure from institute
Deus Caritas Est, ix
diocesan bishops
    ad experimentum incardination of clerical religious as secular priest, 201–204
    authority over institutes, 1–2
    canonical election of major superior of *sui iuris* monastery, 65–69
    changes to institute of diocesan right, authority of bishop *vs.* Apostolic *See*
        regarding, 49–51
    eremitical life in diocese, persons wishing to pursue, 53–56
    extinction or suppression of institute, responsibilities with regard to order's
        decision regarding, 39–43
    finances of institutes, responsibilities regarding, 77–81, 119
    mutuality of relationship between institutes and, viii
    new form of consecrated life, support for and approval of, 61–64
    pontifical right status, diocesan right institutes seeking to obtain, 93, 94
    rest house, notification of bishop of establishment of, 23–26
    universal suffrage for perpetually professed members at chapters, dispensation
        from Constitution to allow, 108
    Virgins, considerations in consecrating persons into Order of, 57–60
    visitations by
        canonical election of major superior of *sui iuris* monastery, diocesan
            bishop's role in, 67
        responsibilities of diocesan bishops regarding, 71–76
diocesan right, institutes of
    alienation of property, 79–81
    changes to, authority of bishop *vs.* Apostolic *See* regarding, 49–51
    Constitutions, changing, 45–48
    erection of, 9–15
    finances, diocesan bishop's responsibilities regarding, 77–81
    pontifical right status, obtaining, 93–95
    visitations, responsibilities of diocesan bishops regarding, 71–76
dismissal or departure from institute

-233-

denial of extension, 177–179
extension of, 171–175, 177–179
imposition of, 181–186
sui iuris monasteries, 143–146
extinction or suppression of institute
diocesan bishop's responsibilities with regard to order's decision regarding, 39–43
"folded" institutes, canonical status of, 157–160

F
federation of religious institutes, requirements for forming, 35–38
finances of institute
alienation of property
diocesan bishop's responsibilities regarding institutes of diocesan right, 79–81, 119
treasurer of institute's canonical obligations regarding, 119–123
diocesan bishop's responsibilities regarding, 77–81, 119
dismissed or departed members, financial assistance for, 219–226
civil lawsuit threats related to, 223–226
members not present in diocese or state, 219–221
refusal to accept indult of dismissal, 221–222
goods of members, cession and renunciation of (*See* cession and renunciation of goods)
members, obligation to support, 157–160
provincial treasurer, canonical advice for, 115–118
forms
ad experimentum incardination of clerical religious as secular priest, 204
alienation of property, letters requesting and granting permission for, 122–123
canonical election of major superior of *sui iuris* monastery, diocesan bishop's letter to Rome regarding, 69
cession, act of, 151
Constitutions, application to change, 20–21
diocesan right, decree of erection of religious institute of, 15
dismissal
decree of, 141, 216–217
petition for confirmation of, 140
warning of potential dismissal from institute due to absence, 139, 212
exclaustration
extension of, 174–175
imposition of, 185–186
federation of religious institutes, requesting and approving, 37–38
marriage as impediment for admission to novitiate, petition for dispensation from, 128–129
parish, agreement between diocese and clerical institute regarding, 7–8

perpetual profession of vows, sanation for irregularities regarding date of, 133
renunciation, act of, 152
separation (marital), decree of, 128
suppression, decree of, 43
transfers between institutes, 169–170

G - I
general chapters. *See* chapters
hermits. *See* eremitical life
Holy See. *See* Apostolic See
impediments
 canonical election of major superior of *sui iuris* monastery, diocesan bishop's
  role in, 68, 69
 novitiate, impediment of marriage for admission to, 125–129
incardination *ad experimentum* of clerical religious as secular priest, 201–204
infirm and elderly religious, voting assistance for, 85–88
institutes. *See also* more specific entries, e.g. clerical institutes, erection of institutes
 absence leading to dismissal from, 135–141, 209–212
 authority of diocesan bishops and Apostolic *See* over, 1–2
 conditions for return to, 177–179
 eremitical life, members wishing to pursue, 53–56
 mutuality of relationship between bishops and, viii
 new form of consecrated life, bishop's support for and approval of, 61–64
 obligations towards members, 157–160
 relationships between members of, 177–179
 transfers between, 165–170
 types of institutes to which cases are applicable, v, viii

L
laicization, departure of member from clerical institute without, 195–199
letter samples. *See* forms
living apart from institute. *See* exclaustration

M
major superiors
 ad experimentum incardination of clerical religious as secular priest, 201–204
 alienation of property by, treasurer of institute's canonical obligations
  regarding, 119–123
 authority of, 83–84
 brother elected as major superior of clerical institute, 89–91
 CICLSAL reporting requirements, general chapter report as satisfaction of,
  97–100
 council, advice and consent of, 101–103
 diocesan bishop's role in canonical election of major superior of *sui iuris*

monastery, 65–69

exclaustration or living apart from *sui iuris* monastery, approval of, 143–146

marriage

cession and renunciation of goods upon entering monastery, 147–152

as impediment for admission to novitiate, 125–129

readmission to clerical institute following death of wife, 205–208

merger or union of institutes

federations, 35–38

obligation to support members of "folded" institutes, 157–160

procedural requirements for, 27–33

N

new form of consecrated life, bishop's support for and approval of, 61–64

novitiates

alienation of property, treasurer of institute's canonical obligations regarding, 119–123

cession and renunciation of goods upon entering monastery, 147–152

federation of religious institutes for purposes of, 35–38

impediment of marriage for admission to, 125–129

O

oratories, responsibilities of diocesan bishops regarding visitation of, 75–76

Order of Virgins

diocesan bishop's considerations in consecrating persons into, 57–60

extinct or suppressed institute members joining, 39–43

Vatican II's revitalization of, 2

ordination and priesthood

incardination *ad experimentum* of clerical religious as secular priest, 201–204

laicization, departure of member from clerical institute without, 195–199

readmission to clerical institute following attempted marriage and death of wife, 205–208

P

papacy. *See* Apostolic See

parishes, clerical religious institutes taking charge of, 3–8

pastoral approach and canonical expertise, importance of combining, v, viii–ix

perpetual profession of vows

date for, 131–134

temporary professed excluded from subsequent profession, 187–190

pontifical right, institutes of

diocesan right institute's change of status to, 93–95

province, changes to Constitutions allowing institute to erect, 17–21

visitations, responsibilities of diocesan bishops regarding, 71–76

postulation. *See* elections and voting

poverty, vow of. *See* cession and renunciation of goods
priests. *See* clerical institutes; ordination and priesthood
proper and universal law, joint consideration of, vii–viii
provinces
    creation of, 17–21
    treasurers of, canonical advice for, 115–118

R
readmission to institute, 191–193, 205–208
region's enhancement to provincial status, 17–21
relationships between members of institutes, 177–179
religious institutes, applicability of cases to, v, viii
renunciation of goods. *See* cession and renunciation of goods
rest house, notification of bishop of establishment of, 23–26

S
sample forms and letters. *See* forms
sanation of irregular date of perpetual profession of vows, 131–134
Second Vatican Council
    diversity introduced to institutional life in light of, viii
    hermits and Order of Virgins, reintroduction of, 2
secular institutes, applicability of cases to, viii
separated status and marriage as impediment for admission to novitiate, 125–129
societies of apostolic life, applicability of cases to, v, viii
special friendships between members of institutes, 177–179
sui iuris monasteries
    canonical election of major superior, diocesan bishop's role in, 65–69
    exclaustration or living apart from, 143–146
    finances, diocesan bishop's responsibilities regarding, 77–81
    visitations, responsibilities of diocesan bishops regarding, 72–75
suppression or extinction of institute
    diocesan bishop's responsibilities with regard to order's decision regarding, 39–43
    "folded" institutes, canonical status of, 157–160

T
temporary professed excluded from subsequent profession, 187–190
transfers between institutes, 165–170
treasurers of institutes
    alienation of property, canonical obligations regarding, 119–123
    provincial treasurers, canonical advice for, 115–118

U
union or merger of institutes

ADDITIONAL RELIGIOUS Law Articles

A select bibliography of seminar articles on various aspect of consecrated life appears the *CLSA Proceedings*, published annually in conjunction with the Canon Law Society of America's convention. Individual issues of *Proceedings* are available from CLSA Publications, PO Box 463, Annapolis Junction, MD 20701. Tel: 301.362.8197 or at clsa@pmds.com.

"Associates and Associations Joined to Religious Institutes," 60 (1998) 132-149, Rose McDermott, SSJ

"Bishops and the Apostolates of Religious," 63 (2001) 49-83, James J. Conn, SJ

"Emerging Expressions of Consecrated Life in the United States: Pastoral and Canonical Implications," 58 (1996) 368-390, Marlene Weisenbeck, FSPA

"Exclaustration," 59 (1997) 267-281, Patrick T. Shea, OFM

"Jurisdiction Exercised by Non-Ordained Members in Religious Institutes," 58 (1996) 292-307, Elizabeth McDonough, OP

"La Protection des Droits dans un Institut Religeux, " 57 (1995) 166-180, Marie-Paule Couturier, FMA

"Models of Participation in Religious Community Chapters," 57 (1995) 181-200, Catherine Darcy, RSM

"Parishes Entrusted to the Care of Religious: Starting Afresh from Christ," 64 (2002) 209-239, Alexander J. Palmieri

"Privacy/Confidentiality Issues in Religious Institutes," 61 (1999) 305-315, Daniel J. Ward, OSB

"Religious Law: Present Reality/Future Possibilities," 65 (2003) 191-212, Patricia Smith, OSF

"Sexual Abuse and Exploitation: Canon and Civil Law Issues Concerning Religious," 67 (2005) 231-240, Daniel J. Ward, OSB

"The Disruptive Religious: Part I. Religious Authority and the Disruptive Religious; Part II. A Focus on the Individual," 66 (2004) 171-194, Elissa A. Rinere, CP & Arthur J. Espelage, OFM

"The Future of Small Religious Institutes: Merging and Other Issues," 57 (1995) 201-215, Marjory Gallagher, SC

"The Personal Patrimony of Individual Members of Religious Institutes: Current Issues," 62 (2000) 263-281, Rosemary Smith, SC

"The Relation Between Religious Institutes and the Diocese," 60 (1998) 82-90, Joanne Graham, OSB

"Visitation in Religious Institutes: A Service of Communion," 61 (1999) 161-178, Sharon L. Holland, IHM

"*Vita consecrata*:   The Post-Synodal Exhortation on Consecrated Life," 58 (1996) 176-186, Doris Gottemoeller, RSM

THE CANON LAW SOCIETY OF AMERICA

Membership in the Canon Law Society of America is open to interested persons who wish to collaborate in the promotion of the pastoral ministry of the Church within the context of its legal/canonical structures. Membership of non-Catholic persons is also welcomed.

The Society's constitution identifies four (4) kinds of membership: Active, Associate, Student, and Honorary. Active membership is open to those who have earned at least a licentiate degree in canon law; active membership is also open to other practitioners in canon law who demonstrate a broadly based competence in canonical issues and who have fulfilled the stipulated requirements established by the Board of Governors of the Society as enumerated in the By-Laws. Associate members are any others who wish to associate themselves with the purpose of the Society. Student membership is open to those enrolled in any school of canon law engaged in studies to obtain a licentiate degree in canon law. Student members enjoy the same prerogatives as associate members in the Society. Honorary members are (a) *ex officio* all the Most Reverend Bishops of the United States, and (b) those persons, who by reason of outstanding contributions in the filed of canon law or in support of the Society, are proposed for this distinction of honorary membership by the Board of Governors and accepted by a majority vote of the active members at the General Meeting.

Membership information and applications are available from the Office of the Executive Coordinator. An application may also be downloaded from the web at www.clsa.org. Payment of the initial dues is required with the submission of the application.

For questions and further information, please contact:

Office of the Executive Coordinator
Canon Law Society of America
108 N Payne Street, Suite C
Alexandria, VA 22314-2906
Tel: 703/739-2560
Fax: 7-3/739-2562
E-mail: coordinator@clsa.org

Roman Replies and CLSA Advisory Opinions

Each year the Canon Law Society of America publishes this annual series as a service to members and the general public. Each issue contains a selection of responses received from various offices of the Holy See on canonical questions and also a collection of brief and practical canonical opinions authored by members of the Canon Law Society of America on a broad spectrum of canonical issues.

Individual issues are available for purchase through CLSA Publications in October of each calender year. Sets of *Roman Replies and CLSA Advisory Opinions* are also available through CLSA Publications. For more information contact:

CLSA Publications
9050 Junction Drive
P.O. Box 463
Annapolis Junction, MD 20701-0463
Tel: 301/362-8197
Fax: 301/206-9789
E-Mail: clsa@pmds.com

For information on payment policy, discount schedule, shipping and handling information, return and replacement policy, please consult www.clsa.org or contact CLSA Publications.

CLSA Advisory Opinions

Since 1982, the Canon Law Society of America by resolution at
its forty-fourth annual business meeting in Hartford, Connecticut,
determined "to establish a committee of canonists to issue
advisory opinions on the mean of the canons of the revised code
after its promulgation." Over the years a broad range of
canonical topics appeared in CLSA Advisory Opinions each
year. Today, there are nearly a thousand entries available to
canonists, religious educators, and parish ministers.

> CLSA Advisory Opinions 1984 – 1993, edited
> by Patrick J. Cogan, S.A. Washington: Canon
> Law Society of America, 1995. ISBN 0-
> 943616-67-0   504 pages.

> CLSA Advisory Opinions 1994 – 2000, edited
> by Arthur J. Espelage, O.F.M. Washington:
> Canon Law Society of America, 2002. ISBN
> 0-9463616-92-1   623 pages.

> CLSA Advisory Opinions 2001-2005, edited
> by Arthur J. Espelage, O.F.M. Alexandria,
> VA: Canon Law Society of America, 2006.
> ISBN 1-932208-11-19   636 pages.

Entries follow the seven books of the Code of Canon Law and
the thirty titles of the Code of Canons of the Eastern Churches.
Entries are organized by canon number as well as by descriptive
title. Entries are updated by the authors where necessary. To
facilitate the use of the texts, there are two cumulative indexes.
The first is by canon number and the second is topical.

Both are designed to be of service to a busy church minister who
needs to research a particular topic or canon.

For more information on the above volumes or all of the